ROUTLEDGE LIBRARY EDITIONS: EDUCATION

DISSEMINATION OF INNOVATION

DISSEMINATION OF INNOVATION

The Humanities Curriculum Project

JEAN RUDDUCK

Volume 241

Routledge
Taylor & Francis Group
LONDON AND NEW YORK

First published in 1976

This edition first published in 2012
by Routledge
2 Park Square, Milton Park, Abingdon, Oxfordshire OX14 4RN

Simultaneously published in the USA and Canada
by Routledge
711 Third Avenue, New York, NY 10017

First issued in paperback 2014

Routledge is an imprint of the Taylor and Francis Group, an informa company

British Library Cataloguing in Publication Data
A catalogue record for this book is available from the British Library

ISBN 13: 978-0-415-50914-5 (Volume 241)
ISBN 13: 978-0-415-75320-3 (pbk)

Publisher's Note
The publisher has gone to great lengths to ensure the quality of this reprint but points out that some imperfections in the original copies may be apparent.

Disclaimer
The publisher has made every effort to trace copyright holders and would welcome correspondence from those they have been unable to trace.

Dissemination of innovation: the Humanities Curriculum Project

Jean Rudduck

Centre for Applied Research in Education
University of East Anglia

Evans/Methuen Educational

First published 1976 for the Schools Council
by Evans Brothers Limited
Montague House, Russell Square, London WC1B 5BX
and Methuen Educational Limited
11 New Fetter Lane, London EC4P 4EE

Distributed in the US by Citation Press
Scholastic Magazines Inc., 50 West 44th Street
New York, NY 10036
and in Canada by Scholastic–TAB Publications Ltd
123 Newkirk Road
Richmond Hill, Ontario

ISBN 0 423 44500 6

Printed in Great Britain by
Richard Clay (The Chaucer Press) Ltd
Bungay, Suffolk

Contents

Preface

This account of the dissemination of the Humanities Curriculum Project has been written retrospectively. As I read through the manuscript I am aware that there emerges a rather tidy picture of a coolly managed process. This is far from the truth. As I looked back, things fell into place, patterns emerged and issues were clarified. At the time things were not as secure as I have made them seem. Missing are the puzzlement and opportunism that characterize such ventures, and the sense of responding to events rather than controlling them.

The account is a history rather than a sociological analysis and it is written from sources which were not originally conceived as data for a study.

I should like to thank those people who have talked to me about their experience of the Project or have allowed me to quote from or describe their work. For the most part their names have not been disclosed in the text and I cannot therefore make a formal acknowledgement. I should also like to thank the Inner London Education Authority for their permission to reproduce in the Introduction an account of the Humanities Project that was first published in their series of occasional papers, *New Educational Developments and Aids to Learning*. I am also grateful to the Open University Press for allowing me to reproduce in Appendix E two profiles from *Problems of Curriculum Innovation I*, edited by Eric Hoyle and Robert Bell.

I should like to acknowledge a debt to my colleagues on the Project team and to Barry MacDonald and his associates on the evaluation team. A group that works closely together for a number of years will tend to take up the ideas of individual members, argue them, explore them, test them, until ultimately, if they prove useful, they become common property. I have greatly benefited from working within a common tradition.

The Schools Council/Nuffield Humanities Curriculum Project was directed by Lawrence Stenhouse and based at Philippa Fawcett College, Streatham, 1967–70, and the Centre for Applied Research in Education, University of East Anglia, 1970–72. Packs of teaching materials on the following themes have been published by Heinemann Educational Books: *Education* (1970), *War and Society* (1970), *The Family* (1970), *Relations between the Sexes* (1970), *People and Work* (1971), *Poverty* (1971), *Law and Order* (1972), and *Living in Cities* (1973).

Introduction

It seemed appropriate, since this book is about dissemination, for the Humanities Curriculum Project to be introduced in an account written by someone who was responding to the experiment as it was disseminated.* Alasdair Aston, an English Inspector, was the HCP contact in the Inner London Education Authority. It is an account which the Project team reprinted for circulation because we respected the grip it had on the issues that seemed to be important in the Project.

* * *

The Humanities Curriculum Project

Areas of study

In 1965, Schools Council Working Paper No. 2 (on raising the school leaving age) † defined the aim of humanities teaching as the forwarding of understanding, discrimination and judgement in the human field. Since 1967, the Humanities Curriculum Project, sponsored by the Schools Council and the Nuffield Foundation, has been conducting research into methods of promoting understanding through humanities teaching and, in particular, has pioneered discussion techniques for handling controversial human issues with adolescent pupils. Adopting from Schools Council Working Paper No. 11 (*Society and the Young School Leaver*, [HMSO] 1967) the idea of areas of enquiry, the Project team, under its director, Lawrence Stenhouse, has turned its attention to nine main areas that can profitably be explored in depth and that are relevant to young people. The study areas developed by the Project are: education, war and society, the family, relations between the sexes, poverty, living in cities, people and work, law and order, race relations.

* A. E. Aston, 'The Humanities Curriculum Project', *New Educational Developments and Aids to Learning* (*NEDAL*), No. 6 (ILEA, 1971).

† *Raising the School Leaving Age: a co-operative programme of research and development* (HMSO, 1965).

Exploration through discussion

Since issues in each of these controversial areas may divide a democratic society, in which individual pupils, teachers and parents will often hold differing opinions, the Humanities Project saw its task as that of promoting open discussion between individuals who hold divergent views and of ensuring that, as far as possible, the views should be thoroughly explored so that they might be responsibly held. It is important to remember that the Project was briefed to pay attention to the needs of pupils in the 14–16 age range who are of average and below average ability, but yet do not experience serious reading difficulties. It is also relevant that, with more and more of the pupils in the age range staying on at school, it has been gradually realized that schools might need to treat these pupils in a more adult way. Hence, several factors seem to have contributed to the Project's emphasis on the pupil's own accountability for his ideas.

Role of the teacher

When a pupil is not responsible for his own ideas, in that he has come to rely overmuch on the guidance of the teacher or of some other 'authority', there is no guarantee that issues will be discussed in depth or that the pupil will properly comprehend where he stands or why he holds his viewpoint. This is partly why the Project has seen humanities teaching as non-instructional in essence, why the students are not encouraged to accept a body of knowledge merely upon authority and why the teacher makes it a point of honour not to state his own viewpoint or to provide any 'answers', in the naïve sense of the term. Whereas, traditionally, teachers have often believed that they can take part in open discussions as equal members with a group of students and that they can participate without imposing their own views, in practice it has been noted that pupils tend to defer to the viewpoint of the teacher, simply because he is a teacher and an adult. Similarly, if teachers look frankly at their own practice in managing the usual run of class discussions, they will observe how frequently they urge towards a consensus of opinion which, consciously or unconsciously, is often a reflection of the teacher's own viewpoint. And, of course, this oblique domination or tendentiousness is not limited to situations in which social issues are being discussed: it is, for example, salutary in this context to listen to pupils responding to literature under the guidance of a teacher who makes his views known, who tells the class 'what the poem is really about'. The Humanities Curriculum Project has therefore sought an enquiry technique that protects the students from the teacher's individual bias, not just because the teacher may indoctrinate in any obvious sense unless there are safeguards, but mainly because the students' views are those that the situation is intended to develop. It is the student's turn to think. In some ways, then, Humanities Curriculum Project teaching, although it operates in the traditional subject areas of English, history, geography, social studies and religious education, can be seen to have aims differing from any academic discipline that sees teaching as the direct, efficient transfer of a recognized body of information.

Many teachers have found it difficult to understand what this shift of emphasis means, the shift from class-instructor to group-chairman. It may seem to some that if they are not directly instructing they are abdicating from their role as educators: they regard it as the teacher's duty to initiate the class into his maturely acquired wisdom. On the other hand, the Project sees the teacher's role as that of the chairman to a discussion group. The chairman by no means abdicates responsibility, in that he watches the standards of learning within the group, he ensures that issues are discussed relevantly and that the views of all members of the group are treated consistently. The teacher, although he is impartial and neutral, will, in fact, be active as a chairman, ensuring that all members of a group can have their say, identifying the issues, providing fresh evidence and resources when these are needed and generally helping the group to find its own way to an understanding of the issues at stake. Often, it will be his responsibility to provide resources that enable the students to explore a controversial area through many media, activities and skills, for discussion is only one aspect of humanities work.

Experience suggests that if the teacher alone determines the direction of a discussion, the students will tend to delegate further responsibility to him or may opt out of exploring the issues for themselves. For this reason, the students are best asked what they wish to discuss. It is generally very unhelpful to the learning situation if the pupils are given an agenda by the chairman or if the chairman has a hidden agenda through which he attempts to steer the discussion. The group will merely attempt to meet teacher-expectation by a kind of guessing game and their understanding of the issues will not be increased. It is all too easy for a teacher to limit the group's exploration by deciding in advance what is going to be discussed, by asking leading questions, by approving only certain responses or by imposing fresh evidence which does not meet the needs of the discussion but which meets his expectation of where the discussion should be going.

Considerable restraint is incumbent on the chairman of the group if the group is going to find its own way to an understanding.

Inspirational teachers, who have gained much satisfaction from teaching and from firing classes with their own enthusiasms, often view the chairman's 'neutrality' with dismay, since positive instruction brings with it the sensation, perhaps illusory, of doing a job well, but experience with the Project suggests that impartial chairmanship can be equally rewarding in that the art of chairmanship is a challenge. Making students responsible for their own learning can be demanding. The chairman may need patience when a group seem to have 'got the wrong end of the stick'. He may have to bite his lip through periods when the group reflect or are in doubt. He will have to remember that it is his duty not to prompt by introducing his own ideas. At times, he may find the pressure hard to bear and this can particularly be the case with a new group who may use silence as a weapon to make him lose his nerve and take on responsibility for the discussion. In the early stages, one determinant of the success of a discussion group may be the chairman's ability to ride the silences until the group begin to offer their views. An over-anxious chairman may not allow the students time to assimilate the evidence, especially if it is printed evidence. However, with a proper allowance of time, the group's offerings usually become more frequent and a point is eventually reached at which controversy emerges. It may then be the chairman's duty to clarify the main differences through questioning and then to throw the discussion open to the whole group by attempting to draw in other members: 'What do other people think?' After a period, the group may decide that they wish to find further information or they may reach a surface agreement. At these moments, the chairman may need to use his knowledge of the Project's packs of evidence so that he can introduce a fresh piece of material to break up an over-easy consensus or force a deeper analysis of the issue under discussion. The chairman ought to be very familiar with the materials in the packs and familiarization takes time. He also has to be very discriminating in the introduction of fresh evidence: it must meet a real need of the discussion.

The materials and facilities

For each of the Project's nine themes, the central team collected a large number of pieces of evidence which were issued for trials to 32 schools * in the United Kingdom. In the light of experience gained, the central team selected for each theme a foundation bank of some 200 pieces of properly

* 36, including 4 Home Office approved schools.

indexed evidence that may take the form of printed matter – reports, extracts, literature, pictures – or taped material. There are also lists of recommended films and film extracts. Evidence is whatever is relevant to the issue under discussion and almost certainly schools and students will find it necessary to supplement the published materials with their own local additions. The published evidence is not intended to carry authority or to represent 'the truth' on any matter: it is merely evidence of the existence of a point of view. Indeed, the evidence has been carefully selected so as to reflect a balanced spectrum of viewpoints. The *War and Society* pack, for example, includes a mediaeval defence of the concept of a just war, as well as facsimiles of letters from the First World War trenches and comments about the situation in Vietnam. The function of the evidence is that of disciplining the discussion. It provides a framework within which views can be exchanged but to treat the evidence as literature or as matter for comprehension is not to make the most of the material.

The Project's materials on the first five themes (*War and Society, Education, The Family, Relations between the Sexes, People and Work*) have been published by Heinemann Educational and are being used in large numbers of schools.* As the Project believes in small-group discussion, the packs contain sufficient evidence for up to twenty students. Each of the 200 items is clearly indexed to aid easy retrieval and the printed materials are stored, twenty strong, in polythene envelopes.

Each pack of theme materials also contains 2 sound-tapes, 2 general handbooks to the project, 2 teachers' sets of all printed evidence and 2 handbooks particular to the pack (e.g. *War and Society*), including lists of films and other resources.

Each pack costs about £37 but a school has also to make regular provision for the Project, in that money is needed for film-hire and may well be needed for outside visits in connection with theme enquiry. Quite apart from money, teachers need space in which to store the packs, rooms in which to hold the chaired sessions, timetable allocations and equipment – especially tape-recorders and film projectors. It is important for the Project that it should receive adequate staffing support (1 teacher to 20 students) and that senior staff are aware of its aims and methods. Teachers in the Humanities team need time for regular meetings so that they can compare experience and discuss problems. It has been found helpful to invite the parents to the school so that they can experience using the

* Packs of material on three more themes – *Poverty, Living in Cities* and *Law and Order* – have since been published.

materials and so that they will understand this particular handling of controversial issues with their children.

In-service training

Above all, the teachers in the participating schools need initial training in the use of the Project's methods and materials. The ILEA induction courses are run by a team of about a dozen teacher-trainers who use videotape and sound recordings to analyse classroom procedures and who regard the Project as a major move in teacher education. Evidence is just beginning to come in from many of our schools that, after some initial floundering, pupils are learning almost for the first time to manage their own work, that writing is developing from the discussions and that young school leavers are becoming well motivated. In fact, as Lawrence Stenhouse has said, 'Experience with the Humanities Curriculum [Project] suggests that in the past we may have tended to underestimate many of our pupils.'

I. The task of dissemination

Within the tradition of our curriculum reform movement, dissemination is about making accessible the insight and experience of a small number of schools as a basis for judgement and response in the system at large. In the Humanities Curriculum Project there were 32 schools, scattered through England and Wales, which gave shape to the ideas of the Project during its experimental phase, 1968 to 1970. As soon as the first public, widespread communication to schools was made in 1969, over 1600 responded with interest. The dissemination task was to be formidable.

Underestimating the task

We have gradually become aware – and partly through American experience – how vulnerable innovations are at the stage of dissemination. Herron[1] identifies the problem:

> For nearly two decades now, we have seen large amounts of capital invested in the production of a variety of new curricula. Unfortunately, evidence is beginning to accumulate that indicates that much of this effort has had relatively little impact on the daily routine of the average classroom teacher. Why? (p. 47)

He goes on to describe the process of extinction: 'a grant expires and an outside consultant or team leaves the scene' and the common occurrence is of 'the new program or project being introduced into a school system and then disappearing without trace.' (p. 47)

In the spring of 1969 the Schools Council organized a conference in Scarborough on curricula for the young school leaver (reported in Working Paper 33).[2] The Humanities Curriculum Project was fairly extensively discussed in the several working groups. At the final plenary session, its director, Lawrence Stenhouse, prophesied that the Project was likely to fail in dissemination for want of adequate provision for training and support. The group dismissed him as a Cassandra. There were public rebukes and private reprimands. The reaction was not, at the time, unusual. There are still vestiges of a touching belief in the notion that good ideas make their own way, although in reality they may not travel even the length of a school corridor:

> Even in those schools where primary experiments have been carried out in selected classes, the experience has not been spread to the rest of the classes! Schools in the same neighbourhood have for a number of years been unaffected by these experiments, and schools in surrounding communities have shown very little interest in them.*

Curriculum innovations that are left to make their own way may travel comfortably for a while on the passport of their distinctive authority, but they are unlikely to survive; without adequate structures for communication and support they will more readily fall prey to teacher mobility, become vulnerable to competing demands and alternative pedagogies, and be more subject to distortion.

The haphazard spreading of ideas we would call diffusion; we would reserve the word dissemination for a policy which is built on a recognition of the difficulties of innovation and which seeks to provide ordered opportunities for communication, training and support.

Misunderstandings complicate the task

The status of the materials

Unlike a marketing approach which aims directly at influence leading to purchase, the dissemination programme of a curriculum project should aim at providing data so that informed decisions may be made by prospective adopters. The achievement of this aim was in our case threatened by the not uncommon view that projects which produce classroom materials are primarily about materials and that the materials are the key to successful implementation in the classroom.

We came to see that the Project would require of most teachers some unlearning and re-learning and that training courses would be a central feature of our dissemination programme. We suspected that it might not be easy to build a climate in which this view would be widely respected. There were several reasons: there was already some evidence of a belief in the magic of materials; the materials of the Project were widely available;

* Per Dalin, in an unpublished paper on the process of innovation in education prepared for a workshop held at St John's College, Cambridge, in 1969. For a report of the workshop see *The Management of Innovation in Education* (OECD/Centre for Educational Research and Innovation, 1971).

there was no mechanism likely to be acceptable to our sponsors by which we could exercise any control so that training might be a prerequisite of purchase.

The Newsom perspective

Common expectation was responsible for the second misunderstanding. The Project was funded as part of the Schools Council's programme in preparation for the raising of the school leaving age. People expected it to fit into the Newsom framework for managing the less able, reluctant student, and expected it to follow the particular lines of Schools Council Working Paper No. 11, *Society and the Young School Leaver.*[3] Both the Newsom Report [4] and Working Paper No. 11 reflect pessimism about the achievement of students: low expectations shape proposed classroom practice and implicitly set limits to classroom attainment. Schools Council Working Paper No. 2, *Raising the School Leaving Age,*[5] on the other hand, presents a different view of students, and it is the thinking of this document that the Humanities Project helps teachers to test in their schools:

> All of this may seem to some teachers like a programme for people who have both mental ability and maturity beyond the reach of most who will leave at the age of 16. The Council, however, thinks it is important *not* to assume that this is so, but rather to probe by experiment in the classroom to find how far ordinary pupils can in fact be taken. (para. 61)

To discover how far pupils can be taken is the central experimental assignment. The Humanities Curriculum Project, then, was not within the Newsom tradition.

Team teaching

The Project used the word 'team' for the group of teachers involved in the Project in any one school. People inferred a team-teaching approach. In fact, early experience of the Project in schools had shown that the form most conducive to reflective enquiry into controversial issues was a small group of students with one teacher as chairman. The 'team', to us, implied a working relationship *outside* the classroom and not a teaching strategy. It signalled that teachers were engaged in a common enterprise, and shared a readiness to discuss experiences and to offer mutual support.

Integrated studies
Warwick in *Integrated Studies in the Secondary School* [6] argues that 'There is, of course, no such thing as Integrated Studies.' (p. 1) The term seems commonly to imply an impulse towards the breaking down of subject barriers in the curriculum. Courses generally represent a fairly large-scale attempt to replace some individually taught subjects with a curriculum unit which draws on these subjects and is a way of transmitting them. The unit is likely to take up a substantial proportion of the timetable. Integrated studies courses are sometimes called 'humanities' courses. The Humanities Project, however, is often introduced in the timetable as an additional or alternative *subject*, filling on average only four to six periods a week. And there are schools where Project work is used as the core of an integrated studies programme. The Project has no concern to break down subject barriers. In the Project handbook [7] the term 'humanities' is discussed in this way:

> We understand by the 'humanities' the arts, religion, history and the behavioural sciences. In the arts, religion and history, personal beliefs and tastes are important and this has implications for the authority of the teacher. Even in the social sciences the theory endorsed by a scholar may often be much more a matter of *personal* conviction than is common in the physical sciences.
>
> This area of the curriculum is extremely susceptible to the problems of alienation. Values and styles are integral to the subject-matter.
>
> The adolescent is at a stage in life when he feels that he is emerging into adulthood and beginning to lay the foundations of his own style, his own value positions, his own personality. The humanities are relevant to this process of maturing. The problem is to make them accessible to the student whose style, values and personality are different from those of his teacher. (p. 4)

This view of what is distinctive in the humanities provided some criteria for the selection of content and for classroom procedures.

The Humanities Project is, in a sense, a form of general studies which finds its logic in a programme of controversial issues. It is concerned more with the application of the disciplines and is not an attempt to teach them.

Intrinsic complications

First, the Project itself is controversial; it divides people and reactions are sometimes quick, strong and emotional. The following verbatim comments are fairly typical of those made at the Project's early open days when the work was introduced to people considering involvement for their schools:

> 'Unsuitable for the average child.'
>
> 'I think there should be an aim they can use.'
>
> 'Knowledge is power and it may well prove that to give pupils knowledge without guidance as to application will give them intellectual constipation.'
>
> 'I would hesitate to accept all the topics as suitable for girls.'
>
> 'We know that society knows right from wrong; we've got to take the risk that pupils will come to right decisions.'
>
> 'What would you do if you found your pupils consistently choosing evil rather than good?'
>
> 'The greatest influences on me have been positively committed people.'
>
> 'Lord Chesterfield's letter – for Newsom pupils?'
>
> 'The material (judging by the specimens) appears to have been selected by people (all young, perhaps) with left-wing views on politics.'
>
> 'It would open windows on life that the so-called non-academic pupil would never see.'
>
> 'It enables the pupils to see the teacher in a more informal light.'
>
> 'I see Humanities Curriculum Project as my salvation. If it doesn't work I'll give up teaching.' (recorded in autumn 1969 by SH, evaluation team, and edited by JR, Project team)*

A task, shared by the Project team and the evaluation team, was to persuade potential users to delay judgement.

Dissemination was further complicated by organizational considerations. Humanities was not a traditional subject in the curriculum of the majority of secondary schools. If there is no existing provision, heads have to make

* Members of the Project and evaluation teams are listed on pp. 172–3.

decisions about finding time for it, finding teachers for it, finding rooms and resources for it – as well as finding ways of talking about it to staff, students and parents. Moreover, if there is no tradition, then there are no internalized standards by which teachers can assess performance and attainment. They may well feel lost. Some schools look to the public examination for standards and status in new curriculum work. This means patient negotiation with examining boards.

The Project requires careful forward planning: it is demanding of resources – half-classes of students, rooms that can be set for discussion, tape-recorders, money for the hire of film, a budget to service the research and creative activities that both feed and grow out of discussion, time for innovating teachers to meet as a team and critically examine their experience.

Although the Project generally fills only a fraction of the timetable, there is evidence that it can have broader repercussions – in attitude and attainment among students, in attitude and approach among teachers. It could be difficult to contain the Project within working walls and working hours; it has a fuller potential, and for some schools this might be a disturbance potential. Heads need to know what they are taking on.

Working Paper No. 2 [5] foresees the possibility of rifts between established values or attitudes within a school and the different values and relationships of the new curricula. There may be dissonance which could foster insecurity among students in an innovating school:

> But adult procedures in the classroon . . . will not be successful if a different kind of relationship between teacher and pupil obtains in the corridor or in extra-curricular activity. If the teacher emphasizes in the classroom his common humanity with the pupils, and his common uncertainty in the face of many problems, the pupils will not take kindly to being demoted to the status of children in other relationships within the same institution. Indeed, they may write off the classroom relationship as a 'soft-sell'. (para. 97)

In short, the Project presents problems in dissemination: people approach it with unhelpful expectations; it has – as do all projects of any substance – a potential for disturbance of institutions and individuals; it is controversial; it necessitates unlearning and re-learning by teachers, and consequently the organization of opportunities for training and support; it is not an established area of the curriculum; it is demanding of human and material resources.

Responsibilities defined

By 1969, the Project team was trying to alert decision-makers to the problems of dissemination. Papers were prepared for a meeting of LEA representatives in May; some were intended also for distribution to heads. They carried, like today's cigarette packets, consumer warnings. The cover page of a paper on the organization of the Project in schools which was distributed to heads included the following passages:

> There may be schools which would be ill-advised, either because of the traditional ethos of the institution or because of its particular stage of development, to become involved in the kind of experiment which the Project offers. All schools should be aware of its implications for change: more immediately in the role of the teacher and his relationship with pupils; ultimately, in the definition of authority and in the way it relates to individual responsibility, both within and outside the school. . . .
>
> The paper assumes that an interested head has already considered the general appropriateness of the Project for his school in terms of:
>
> **1** the authoritarianism of the system within the school and whether the ethos and attitudes are open or conducive to change, or resistant to it;
>
> **2** any reorganizational upheavals and whether uncertainty is such that research and innovation would be too precariously based;
>
> **3** his commitment to the general aims of the Project and his concern for the group of pupils for whom the Project is intended so that teachers would be working against a background of understanding and support. (JR, Project team, 1969)

To sum up: the team saw its responsibility in dissemination in terms of providing opportunities for people to obtain adequate information about the Project and its implications, especially about its implications for different settings; of ensuring that training courses were both highly regarded and widely available; and of identifying the different kinds of support that innovating teachers would need if the work were to survive as a creative force. But the Project also saw that if the work were to survive independently of the development team, then others – teachers, teachers' centre leaders, local authority and college personnel – must share respect and responsibility for dissemination and become competent in its practice.

Few, if any, curriculum projects which started life in the 1960s had an element of dissemination built into their original design. The Humanities Project was granted an extension of time and money for evaluation and dissemination. How did it set about its task of communication, training and support?

II. Shaping a strategy for dissemination, 1969–70

Plan and counter-plan

First thoughts and competing tasks

Dissemination crept into the agenda of Project staff meetings in January 1969 – four months after the experimental work had begun in schools. At that time responsibility for its organization had not been allocated. The following passage from the minutes of a staff meeting on 22 January shows (items 12, 13, 14, 16, 21, 22 and 29) what form the first stirrings took. It also shows the range of competing demands that can confront a team (we were then eight, with an evaluation officer) that attempts a holistic approach to curriculum development: *

> *Forward planning.* Lawrence [the director] thought it was time to look afresh at the structure and organization of the Project and to decide on what its priorities were. It was decided that the best way to do this might perhaps be to give everyone a couple of minutes to write down their own priorities and then to make a list of these. This was done:
>
> 1. the theoretical unity of the staff;
> 2. to help schools with the interpretation of the Project's experimental design;
> 3. support for problem schools, including better delivery of materials;
> 4. preparation of a videotape of Project work in classrooms;
> 5. teachers' centre meetings for Project schools;
> 6. the study of promising schools;
> 7. the relationship between the Project and other relevant work/projects;
> 8. the preparation of materials;
> 9. the preparation of research reports (as distinct from evaluation reports);
> 10. outside consultancy on materials;
> 11. evaluation;

* The Project shorthand has been expanded slightly to make the passage more accessible.

12. informing LEAs, and the relationship with LEAs;
13. colleges of education and universities;
14. speaking about the Humanities Curriculum Project in contexts relevant to Project needs;
15. design of storage and retrieval systems;
16. CSE planning;
17. helping schools with the interpretation of the teaching situation;
18. skills of members of Project team in relation to needs of schools;
19. patterns of school organization of the Project;
20. continuity of support for schools after the Project ends;
21. feedback for modifying packs;
22. the film-hire problem – continuity in diffusion stage;
23. the possibility of moving into other experimental schools, and criteria for doing so;
24. helping teachers with a strategy for using materials and developing follow-up work;
25. a policy for heads;
26. parents;
27. censorship;
28. clarifying the roles of team members;
29. postponing publication;
30. dropping experimental schools that don't meet their commitments to the Project;
31. a close look at [Penguin] *Connexions*.

Identifying the agencies of dissemination

We had first to decide whether we should work through colleges of education, teachers' centres or LEAs – or whether we should concentrate on all three:

> The overall aim was to establish, by 1972, sufficient people throughout the country with understanding and energy enough to ensure that the experiment could be sustained, that new people could be effectively brought in, that experiences could be shared and learned from, that standards could be constantly rethought. (internal unpublished paper, *Diffusion * and the HCP*, JR, Project team)

* It was not until 1971 that the evaluation team, aware of Hoyle's discussion of the two concepts,[8] raised the question of terms with the Project team; thereafter, consistent use was made of the term 'dissemination'.

Colleges had a network of schools in their training areas; they could offer some in-service work but they could also introduce teachers in pre-service courses to the Project's working style. This seemed too slow and uncertain a process to enable the Project to make a substantial contribution to planning for the raising of the school leaving age. On the other hand, curriculum courses in colleges might manage to communicate something of the theoretical framework of the Project.

Teachers' centres were not strong contenders. Their growth over the country was patchy and their role too variously interpreted to make them a reliable kingpin of a dissemination programme. In any case, we saw them as an instrument or extension of local authority activity.

We decided to work through LEAs. The decision was rationalized in this way:

> It seemed appropriate that in-service training should be the major emphasis in diffusion and that LEAs should be the major agency of diffusion. We needed an agency with knowledge of schools, of local resources, with financial and organizational powers to give appropriate support. Underlying this decision is the recognition that diffusion could be more effective if it shaped itself according to local needs, resistances and resources. (internal paper, *Diffusion and the HCP*, JR, Project team)

The working assumption that LEAs knew their schools turned out to be far from the truth.

From the outset, then, we expected LEAs to take responsibility for responding to interest in the Project shown by their schools (and indeed for making schools aware of a new curriculum possibility) and for building some reliable mechanism for ensuring continuity of development locally when the Project officially ended. By late 1970, the role of the local authority was more clearly defined:

> Each interested LEA will, it is hoped, think about disseminating information, building a training team, sending its trainers to a centrally organized course, conducting local introductory and training meetings, and planning an 'after-care' programme of meetings for teachers so that they can develop their study of their work by sharing problems, experiences and insights. (circular to LEAs, JR, Project team)

We first encountered response to the role that we were slowly shaping for our LEA contacts at a conference in London on 29 May 1969. It was attended by contacts from 27 of the 30 pilot LEAs. Major anxieties expressed by the contacts included the lack of appropriate preparatory work in schools, the organizational requirements of the Project, and the identification of teachers capable of handling the programme. What was missing at the meeting were signs of expertise in the tactics of dissemination. We had certain expectations:

> At this stage we're not offering a plan of diffusion but rather asking for advice from the LEAs. (staff meeting minutes, April 1969)

But we were given little advice by our local authority consultants. Our expectation was naïve, dissemination was a new notion. Moreover, LEAs differ so markedly that it would be difficult to extract anything but the most general statement of procedure from a large group of their representatives. Individual interviews, instead, might have given us a useful insight into the various configurations of local problems and possibilities.

The plan

We eventually evolved a strategy for dissemination in which the insights of the Project and the evaluation team were pooled. The gamble was on numbers: we had no firm idea what the magnitude of response would be.

The dissemination calendar moves forward and backward from the publication date of May 1970. The first official letter had gone out in May 1969. It was sent from the Schools Council to all Directors of Education and Chief Education Officers, and invited a response. The details of the dissemination policy were only lightly drawn:

> In order to make possible the most effective use of these materials, the Project team will offer training courses to those who will train the schoolteachers, and these courses will draw upon the experience of the thirty-two experimental schools. The training courses will be available from 1970 onwards. . . . *As far as possible they will be conducted within the areas of co-operating authorities.* [my italics]

The Project followed up the idea of co-operation in a letter to all the LEAs who had by then responded to the Schools Council circular:

> We must work towards a diversified rather than a standardized pattern of training. (LS, Project team, July 1969)

But there were signs of nervousness in the letter:

> It is already clear that the response will be a heavy one. . . . The task facing us is complicated by the weight of response and by the diversity of proposals received from LEAs.

The nervousness had actually set in earlier:

> Jean is to deal with the increasing number of requests for information from LEAs. There are a number of problems here and a looming strain on staff resources. (staff meeting minutes, June 1969)

The counter-plan

Before the end of July we had abandoned the first plan, which was to train trainers by setting up a series of smallish courses in areas formed by clusters of interested LEAs. We decided instead to hold three large, central training courses and to invite LEA teams of trainers to come to these.

We had underestimated the patient labour involved in encouraging adjacent LEAs (with different understandings of the function of the courses and of the character of the Project) to organize a joint training enterprise: to agree time, place, duration, financial commitment, leadership. Nor, given the actual weight of the response from LEAs, could our team have covered the ground had we gone ahead with the original plan. Moreover, the settings would have varied in quality; we could not have guaranteed that there would be rooms appropriate for small-group meetings, videotape facilities and so on. The large, central courses would have advantages: the provision of resources and the standard of comfort were likely to be better, the impact was likely to be greater, and the opportunity for exchanging ideas with people from a wide range of schools was likely to be more stimulating.

So conferences were booked for Easter 1970 and a 'revised note on diffusion' was sent to all LEAs in July 1969. This note made the following points about training:

training is difficult and the 'best people available should be included in the LEA training team';

the team should include at least one LEA representative;

an LEA–HCP contact should be nominated who would have responsibility for communication and for the organization of the local programme;

the LEA team would, after attending the central training course, induct teachers locally 'in whatever way seems most appropriate'; these local courses would take place between May and September 1970;

the LEA team should study the experiment in local schools and give support to teachers;

the pattern of the local courses would be discussed at the central training courses at Easter.

The letter also invited LEAs to send representatives to one of the series of open days, arranged for the autumn of 1969 as introductions to the Project.

Informing the schools

No initial communication went direct from the Project team, nor from the Schools Council, to schools. In May/June 1969, the Project's publisher, Heinemann Educational Books, circularized all secondary schools in England and Wales (later in Scotland) and all other relevant educational institutions. The communication included a pre-paid postcard which schools requiring further information about materials and about training were invited to send back. Heinemann forwarded these to the Project headquarters. We received well over 1600. We sent out semi-standardized letters giving details of the LEA's dissemination plans (if known) and the name of the LEA's HCP contact (if known). We also sent out an attractive brochure which gave basic information about the Project, emphasized the importance of training for teachers and suggested some organizational pre-conditions for introducing the Project in schools. (On all issues of introduction and organization, it was our policy to flag what seemed to be significant factors for a decision and to stress, given the variation in contexts, that people had to take responsibility themselves for the details of their implementation designs.)

We had decided to inform LEAs which schools had returned the pre-paid postcard so that they would know the size and pattern of possible dissemination activity in their areas. There were difficulties – and one major oversight: Heinemann had omitted to ask schools to cite their LEA in addition to giving their name and address. The identification task was laborious and we made mistakes – 124 misplaced schools from 61 LEAs.

We noted how smartly an LEA would respond to our letter when we had made an error:

> I cannot think which member of the Schools Council team can have determined that the B—— Girls School is in the London Borough of X.

A circular letter of apology was promptly prepared. We took pains not to cross LEAs nor to let an impression of incompetence go unexplained. Too much was at stake.

Names of schools apparently interested in the Project were forwarded to LEAs with comments – to LEAs which had already expressed firm interest in dissemination:

> You may wish to make contact with these institutions about training programmes;

and to LEAs which had made no response, a veiled threat:

> I am sending you these details of response from your area because we think it essential that a team of teachers in any school wishing to buy the materials and to develop the work along the lines explored by the Project should attend some training course. You might like to consider the implications of these expressions of interest – which are of course tentative at this stage. (JR, Project team, August 1969)

The information was variously regarded by LEAs. Some saw it as a useful means of containing the experiment and they followed up only the named schools. Other LEAs interpreted the expression of interest by some schools as a signal for a thorough local information campaign among all schools. At this stage we noted that whereas some LEAs took into consideration the opinions of schools before making a decision about a local dissemination programme, others planned a programme and then sought the support of schools.

The policy of informing LEAs about potentially interested schools provoked a handful of irate or aggrieved letters from heads: they had returned the pre-paid card to Heinemann without being genuinely interested in the experiment and had subsequently been approached by their LEA about participation. We were accused of a breach of trust.

The pilot schools *

Our team resources were stretched to the full in 1969. By August 25, we had reconsidered at a staff meeting the allocation of responsibilities within the team in order to ensure that both our pilot-school responsibilities and our dissemination responsibilities were met. In October 1969 we contacted our thirty-two pilot schools, outlining the dissemination strategy and warning them of their possible role:

> Teachers in our present experimental schools may well be called upon by their authorities to give information or advice to interested schools in their area. They may also be asked to assist with the training programme in some way. It would be helpful if I could have a note of the ways in which teachers are being asked to help so that I can keep a full picture of the pattern of diffusion. (JR, Project team)

It was important to avoid the situation where pilot schools felt that they were now of secondary interest. Indeed, the significance of their work was at its highest in this, the second year of the experiment, and we were concerned to increase our capacity for studying their work. (We were also planning a final conference exclusively for the pilot schools.)

The Project team

The Project team was not altogether happy with the dissemination programme. We were pessimistic about people's capacity to understand the nature of the experiment:

> MP asked what would be the frame of mind of teachers about to embark on the Project. JR said complete ignorance would be the only safe assumption. LS said teachers would have one of three reasons for being at the training courses: they would have been pushed by the LEA into adopting the Project, or they would have been pushed by the headmaster, or a group of teachers would have pushed the headmaster into it. He added that they would be looking for a simple solution to their problems which would avoid the need for radical change. (staff meeting minutes, 7 July 1969)

* The Project team in fact used the word 'experimental' (see Chapter VIII, p. 90).

We were already concerned about LEAs' understanding of our training strategy:

> Lawrence said that LEAs didn't seem to grasp the idea that the Project wants to train personnel to train teachers, and not to train teachers directly. (staff meeting minutes, 7 July 1969)

Scepticism about achieving effective communication became intense and by the autumn its force was reflected in the advice of the evaluation officer, Barry MacDonald:

> Barry suggested that the team might review its diffusion programme in the light of its experience, and consider the possibility of an alternative programme which would permit a greater degree of quality control than is at present feasible. (staff meeting minutes, 27 October 1969)

We did not think it possible to mount an alternative induction at this stage – what was needed was a co-ordinated, large-scale induction for LEAs and heads and senior teachers in the management of educational innovation – but we did review the problems. These included the plight of interested schools in authorities which had responded negatively to the Project and where there would be no organized training and support; uncertainty whether Heinemann could meet its May publication deadline (it was crucial to have published materials at the local training courses which would start in early summer); the provision of opportunities for training and support for non-maintained secondary schools (independent schools, Home Office approved schools and Army schools).

We decided to concentrate our efforts on careful planning of the central training courses, the clarification of their function and the provision of fuller information for LEAs. By November we had prepared a bundle of papers for LEAs who were contemplating participation in a dissemination programme:

Paper A: some guidance for the forward planning of locally organized training courses;

Paper B: notes on the organization of the Project in schools;

Paper C: information about the purchase of materials;

Paper D: information about hire and purchase of recommended films: 'Film hire in diffusion will present problems which cannot be solved unless distributors are prepared to make more copies available. Widespread hiring could cause a bottleneck.'

We also planned a second round of central training courses, and agreed to provide information about them as early as possible. These might accommodate LEAs who had been slow to respond initially, and individual schools in areas where there was no LEA programme of involvement.

So ended our planning for the stages leading to what we hoped would be the attendance of well-informed teams of local trainers at our three central courses at Easter 1970 and the subsequent induction of groups of teachers locally by the nucleus training teams.

III. Developing the strategy for dissemination, 1970-72

Facts and figures

The activities of 1969 and early 1970 constituted our largest dissemination thrust. After the first round of training courses was over, the need for information days continued, but they were attended more and more by teachers from individual schools and less by LEA representatives. Altogether we have held about 30 open days and about 1000 people have come to them. The pattern has remained virtually unchanged: we talk about the development, aims, strategy and effects of the Project, about the materials, about introducing the Project into schools and LEAs, and we allow time for questions and discussion. Latterly we have shown videotapes of the Project in the classroom.

We held three centrally organized and, as an alternative strategy, two local and two regionally organized courses * during the first phase of dissemination in 1970. In 1971 and 1972 we held three centrally organized courses. In 1970, 272 people came to the central courses (in addition, approximately 100 were at the four alternative strategy courses); in 1971, 124 people came to the courses, and in 1972, 150 people (see Appendix A for fuller details). In the three years of dissemination, therefore, we have trained, at courses organized by members of our team, over 600 people.†

The first public communication about the dissemination of the Project was the Schools Council letter of May 1969 (see p. 24). Ninety-three

* The alternative strategies involved 17 LEAs. Each of the four courses was led by members of the central Project team:

(*a*) an extended course of weekly meetings, with one residential weekend, for teachers' centre leaders, heads and teachers in a county authority;

(*b*) an intensive course in a very large urban authority;

(*c*) an extended course of weekly meetings for a region that already had a working structure (the North West Regional Curriculum Development Project);

(*d*) an intensive course for two adjacent authorities that had applied too late to secure places on the three main training courses. These LEAs were close at hand to the Project team's headquarters.

† We have restricted our analysis to the period of the Project funding. In fact, training courses continued to be held, centrally, after 1972.

LEAs responded positively to this letter. Not all were interested in immediate involvement and 82 sent representatives to the first training courses. Most of these had earlier sent representatives to an information day. In 1971, people from an additional 30 LEAs came to the courses (there were few formally constituted 'teams' as there ostensibly were at the first round of courses). In 1972, an additional 4 LEAs were represented at our courses but only one sent a nominated 'team'.

Of the 65 LEAs that were represented at our three major training courses in 1970, 18 teams came without an LEA representative who would, according to our earlier communication, take responsibility for the detailed co-ordination of the work in his area. The larger the team and the greater the cost of sending it to the conference, the more likely it was to have an LEA officer in its number. Teachers at these courses were dissatisfied at the lack of briefing and showed marked uncertainty about role and responsibility. Members of some training teams had not met each other before the conference and had no idea that a training function was on the cards. The surprise that followed our first address to the group as 'potential trainers' created an undercurrent of distrust that was partly directed towards the Project and partly towards the local authorities.

Revisions and reflections

The experience of the first centrally held training courses enabled us to give more specific advice to LEAs who had expressed interest in the second and third cycles of communication, training and support planned for 1971 and 1972. We drew up a schedule of events leading to the training course and made an analysis of basic patterns of LEA approaches to training. In detail these approaches would, and should, vary from area to area according to local needs, policy and resources, but our notes might, we hoped, serve as a foundation for thinking:

Activities leading to training courses and implementation in schools

As a result of the experience of the first phase of dissemination 1969/70 we would recommend the following skeleton of preliminary activities:

1 LEA representatives to an open day;
2 introductory meetings within authority for heads of secondary schools;

3 provisional booking for training courses;
4 more detailed discussion with teachers and heads from schools firmly interested as a result of **2**;
5 selection of trainers and final booking;
6 briefing sessions for trainers and first planning of locally organized training courses to be held after the centrally organized courses.

Composition of training teams and approaches to local training

The constitution of the nucleus training team and its subsequent strategy for introducing the Project to other teachers in the area will largely be determined by the authority's initial decision to work to one of three basic patterns of dissemination. (There may well be others but these [three] have emerged fairly clearly during the first phase of dissemination and may serve as a basis for LEA planning.)

Pattern 1

A small but very strong team of trainers (perhaps including LEA inspectors or advisers, and/or teachers' centre leaders, and/or college lecturers and/or practising teachers) would attend the Easter training course and then run introductory courses for all teachers likely to be involved in the work in the interested schools in the area. This local course might be centrally organized, or, in a larger authority, parallel courses might be run at a number of teachers' centres. The courses might be short-term intensive, or extended in a series of weekly meetings. This nucleus team would, in addition to conducting introductory courses, be responsible for maintaining some sort of support (for example, meetings to exchange experiences and explore common problems and insights) for teachers starting on the experiment.

Pattern 2

Firmly interested schools might be identified fairly early on and the training team might consist of one very carefully chosen teacher from each of the schools committed to trying the experiment. These teachers would be recognized as leaders of the Humanities team in their schools and, after attending the centrally organized course at Easter, would teach-in, in their schools, the remaining members of the Humanities teams. The head would need to have a full understanding of the timetabling implications of this pattern of dissemination. After the within-school training, the various teams of teachers working on the Project would need to meet to exchange experiences and discuss the experiment along the lines of the support pattern outlined in **1** above.

PATTERN 3

Where an authority is taking the initiative in innovation and is anxious to start the experiment on a very small scale – say in one pilot school – all the teachers likely to be involved in that school might be sent to the central Easter course. Should it be decided, after study of the experiment in the one school, that the work could usefully be extended, these teachers might take responsibility for introducing the approach to other schools in the area.

Whichever of these patterns an authority might choose to work to, we would hope that at least one member of the LEA personnel would attend the Easter training courses at the University of East Anglia and would act as co-ordinator of the local team and as main contact with the Project central team. (JR, Project team, 1970)

Timing in these guidelines was determined by the need to allow for attendance at a spring training course, a period of local training, and a September start to the Project in schools. They were intended for LEAs which were, for the first time, making a co-ordinated attempt at the local introduction of HCP. Our autumn courses, on the other hand, were timed primarily to provide training opportunities for teachers who had recently joined a school where the Project was already under way and who could not attend a local induction course.

We had laboured affectionately over these new, empirically based guidelines but had missed the rhythm of LEA response. The time of the 'team' was over; the 1971 and 1972 courses were characterized by the attendance of teachers from individual schools and colleges. Our experience would suggest that LEAs, are likely to be most influenced by the first impact of dissemination opportunities. Thereafter, the paler image of the project, without the status of introductory letters from the Schools Council and glossy information leaflets from the project team, does not compete effectively against either established or new demands for LEA attention and money. Although LEAs might be willing to support individual initiatives from teachers, they are unlikely to take initiatives for the organized introduction of the project once the first dissemination phase is over.

A comparison of the participants at the first course, in March 1970, and at the course in September 1972 (the ninth) shows the trend towards fragmentation (see Table 1). At the 1971 and 1972 courses there were

Table 1 Participants compared at first and ninth central training courses, March 1970 and September 1972

Participants	*1970 Course 1*	*1972 Course 9*
Teachers	72[a]	53[b]
LEA advisers and teachers' centre leaders	25	5
Further education lecturers	—	4
College of education lecturers	1	—
University lecturers	—	1
Others	—	6[c]
Total no. of participants	98	69

[a] From maintained schools in 23 LEAs

[b] From maintained schools in 33 LEAs, 1 private and 1 Home Office approved school

[c] Teachers from schools in Scotland, Eire and the USA; lecturers from universities in Northern Ireland, Australia and New Zealand

many teachers from LEAs that had sent a team to the first round of courses – sometimes because the local training courses had not got off the ground, sometimes because the local nucleus needed new blood, sometimes because individual schools where the Project was reasonably strong chose to have new HCP teachers inducted centrally rather than locally, and sometimes because teachers had taken the initiative in applying for a place at a course and had not known that other schools in their authority were doing the Project and that there might be induction courses available locally. Other teachers came from schools in areas where there were no imminent opportunities for local induction and support.

The fact that the 1971 and 1972 courses were largely attended by school rather than LEA representatives may also have been the result of our method of advertising: in 1969, booking details were sent almost exclusively to HCP contacts in LEAs; schools that applied independently for places were required to assure us that their activity was in fact part of an organized plan recognized by the authority:

> If you will be supporting yourselves at the training course, I should like to know how your starting the work relates to the work in the authority. (letter from JR, Project team, November 1969)

Thereafter we relaxed our policy and in 1971 and 1972 we advertised more widely – in the *Times Educational Supplement* and in the Project's *Evaluation Report,* which was sent direct to schools.

Our recognition of the shifting clientele for our courses, and of our need to modify their focus, is reflected in our 1970, 1971 and 1972 descriptions of the training courses:

> *1970*
> The Project team will induct a nucleus of trainers chosen by the authority; this nucleus will then train the teachers from the authority's experimental schools. It is highly desirable that all members of an authority team attend the same course but this is not absolutely essential. While it would be helpful to have some indication of response fairly early on, we would not wish authorities in any way to rush the choice of people who will form their training team.
>
> *1971*
> The courses are mainly designed to meet the needs of teachers' centre leaders and LEA personnel who seek an understanding of the Project as a basis for their planning of local patterns of communication, training and support for interested teachers. They are also for teachers or lecturers who, as individuals, are primarily interested in introducing the Project into their own schools or colleges.
>
> *1972*
> People coming to the course will generally be thinking about introducing the Project into their own schools or colleges. Some may also be concerned with introducing the experiment to other teachers as part of the locally organized programme of training and support. Towards the end of the course we shall discuss the general problems of communication and look at the ways in which different areas of the country have responded.

> Course members will come from a variety of settings: they will include teachers, lecturers in colleges of education and further education, teachers' centre leaders and LEA personnel. (JR, Project team)

The test of the effectiveness of our dissemination policy is whether responsibility has been taken, locally, for setting up some recognizable framework for supporting teachers who are involved in or interested in the Project. No clear evidence emerges from a study of local authorities; the pattern of response is very varied. In some areas the Project and its local team died together and then, in some of these, it rose again, phoenix-like, from its own ashes; in other places, the local team provided a robust focus for experimental work, a focus strong enough to survive changes in the original nucleus team. In yet other areas it has been an individual, not a team, who has built programmes of induction and support; in others again, sporadic interest from scattered schools has sometimes stayed alive, and sometimes faded from lack of support before it has had a chance to translate itself into action.

Clearly, for some areas, dissemination was a failure. This failure might be interpreted in two ways: it could be a criticism of our dissemination strategy as unrealistic in its demands or of the system for its inability to make coherent responses to the opportunities provided by the Nuffield Foundation and the Schools Council's programme of work.

Criticism of the Project's strategy raises the issue of control. We had no control over the published materials; any institution could buy them if it wished, and for any purpose. Secondly, we might have exercised tighter control over our training programme, granting places on courses only to LEA teams that showed evidence of understanding the need for co-operative preparation and could present a coherent plan for a support structure. But as long as LEA involvement in any project's dissemination programme remains optional, such a policy would be unfair to individual schools. We tried to control through words rather than restrictive practices, through cautionary notes – and later, as evaluation findings became available to us, cautionary tales – rather than through sanctions.

The need now is to understand what stood in the way of effective management, at local level, of the Project's dissemination strategy, and to speculate about structures that would enable the local authority system as a whole to respond deliberately, coherently and productively to the possibilities of innovation.

IV. Problems in LEA response

There was no uniformity of LEA response to the dissemination of the Humanities Curriculum Project, but in retrospect patterns did emerge (see Appendix B: Profiles of response in three local authorities). Our interest in these patterns outstripped our capacity to study them but the evaluation team was able to explore some of the issues. We need to know more precisely what factors contribute to particular styles of response and what implications these have for the short- and long-term dissemination of a project.*

With a new breed of LEA institutions – the teachers' centre – and a new strain of LEA personnel – the Curriculum Development Officer – one might be beguiled into believing that dissemination would be handled fairly consistently from area to area. But this is not so. In fact, the superstructure for response to innovation rests on personnel and institutions that are only nominally similar. There can – and should be – no masterplan for the dissemination of a project. LEAs are intrinsically different.

Variation in response is partly due to a set of innate features: size of LEA, geographical position, basic income, number of schools and their geographical relationship to teachers' centres and colleges of education. Then there are the acquired features: the number of advisory staff, personalities, perception of role in innovation, financial policy, dissemination policy (if any), the existence of a project pilot school in the area. Bridging the two categories are experience and traditions. An example of a tradition would be the readiness among teachers in a large rural authority, where schools are scattered, to travel thirty miles or so to a teachers' centre meeting. Such a readiness – with the certainty of the LEA meeting travel costs – makes possible a continuing support system for innovating teachers in the area.

Decisions and issues

LEAs considering local involvement in the dissemination of the Project

* For an exploration of some of the issues raised in this chapter, see also S. Humble and J. Rudduck, 'Local education authorities and curriculum innovation' in *Problems of Curriculum Innovation I*, ed. Hoyle and Bell.[8]

were presented with several areas of decision: to respond or not to respond to the opportunity for organized activity; to shape a pattern of response that was appropriate to the local policy, needs and resources; to determine the extent of and conditions for financial investment; to determine where responsibility for action would lie. More specifically, we had invited LEAs to nominate a Project contact, to present information about the Project to schools, and to select and brief a local dissemination team: in short, to plan a coherent programme of communication, training and support that could exist independently of the Project's central team.

It is probably true that in 1969 we were asking LEAs to undertake responsibilities that went beyond their experience. The Project was not offering experts who would come in and run the dissemination show but was, instead, asking LEAs to develop their own resources and expertise. It is not surprising that there were uncertainties and anomalies in the early years of dissemination.

Support for the involvement of schools in the Project

Support generally involves money.* In the period from 1969, LEA marginal money (discretionary funds for curriculum development, for instance) was scarce. LEAs were not in a position to provide support for the local involvement of schools on all nationally or regionally developed projects that became available. Decisions had to be made. Geoff Collins, an assistant inspector of schools (now a headmaster) and HCP contact during the early dissemination of the Project, described the problem at a 1971 Schools Council conference on 'Teachers Centres and the Developing Curriculum' in Clacton (his paper was reprinted in *Dialogue*):[9]

> Available funds for curriculum development are limited, however, and the adviser is often forced to make indefensible selections for financial support between school X wishing to start the Integrated Studies Project, school Y wishing to buy materials for the General Studies Project, and four primary schools wishing to buy *Breakthrough to Literacy* materials. (p. 16)

Since there is generally no structure within LEAs by which externally developed projects are examined and presented to the scrutiny of teachers, it follows that LEA personnel make the decisions about which projects will be handled locally in their dissemination phase. In 1967, LEAs were

* The issue of financial support is discussed more fully in Chapter VII, pp. 71–3.

widely enthusiastic for involvement in the pilot phase of projects – this was the first wave of a national curriculum development movement. In the period 1970–72 there was something of a cloud-burst of nationally sponsored projects. By 1973, LEA personnel, asked about involvement in a 'new project', were likely to make jaded replies: 'We have fourteen projects in one school already'. Projects compete for money, time and attention. How are choices and priorities determined? By whom, and on what criteria?

We had some evidence about decision-making, but on a very narrow front, from the response of a group of LEAs in the areas where the Keele Integrated Studies Project was located. The Keele Project and the HCP are built on different assumptions and exemplify different patterns of partnership between materials and method. They could be said to be alternatives. In practice they are competitors. The competition is largely the result of the limited financial resources available for innovation but it was intensified, in the Keele Area Training Organization (ATO) area by the design of the Keele project: a group of LEAs had established a commitment to the Project by making a financial investment in the early stages of its development. Hence the tenor of the responses from those LEAs to the first Humanities Project dissemination letter that went to all Directors of Education and Chief Education Officers in May 1969:

> A number of our schools are already involved in the Keele Project and it is likely that many more will be involved in the near future if present developments materialize as planned. . . . I do not think that the authority's schools would wish to be involved in both these projects in view of the confusions that might arise and I am sure you will appreciate that it would be better for them, at present anyway, to restrict their activities to the Keele Project. (Chief Education Officer, July 1969)

The point is a very simple one: where decisions are made at CEO level about the authority's involvement in one project rather than another, the teachers' access, locally, to information and support for the rejected project will clearly be restricted. In short, LEA decisions of this kind limit the repertoire of possibilities open to teachers in so far as these possibilities are unlikely to be effective in the classroom without a background of training and support.

In fact the Project team was not able systematically to collect data on the decision-making process in LEAs. Shreds of evidence tended towards the sensational. They were certainly not generalizable:

> Mr X and Mr Y (general advisers) said that the secondary science vote was £14 000 per year whereas the vote for secondary arts was only £12 000. They saw the HCP as a means of redressing the balance. (report by JR, Project team, 1971)

External factors – the reputation of the sponsors, the size of their investment in the Project, expectations of the Project's contribution to raising the school leaving age programmes – may have influenced decisions about involvement. What emerges is the difficulty of presenting a project to decision-makers in such a way that judgements may be made, at least in part, on intrinsic factors, such as the potential of a project for the development of research competence in teachers. One question became increasingly important: do LEAs have a policy for the betterment of schools that will provide criteria for the investment of time, money and personnel?

It is probably fair to say that action response is likely to be faster when responsibility for decision-making lies with an individual rather than with a democratic, participatory or committee structure. A policy for curriculum development, while honouring the everyday realities of limited money and manpower, would provide criteria for the individual decision-maker; through it he would be accountable to his colleagues in the LEA offices and in the classrooms. A controversial project tends to divide people. A policy is some safeguard that personal judgement rather than personal prejudice will guide decisions about the giving of official LEA backing to an experiment. There was evidence that certain decisions made by individual officers cut interested teachers off from the support they needed to implement the Project in their school:

> Mr X's [the Assistant Education Officer's] decision that Anonshire should not take part in the Project scheme would certainly be a final decision but naturally those of us involved in curriculum work will always continue to be interested in your work and its development. (letter from a teachers' centre leader, 1970)

Was there the germ of a well-controlled tension in this gentle and obedient letter? The following extract is from a letter by a Chief Education Officer printed in a widely read educational journal:

> I would suggest that any officer or elected member who had a school involved in the Humanities Curriculum Project, for instance, should

> have a look at the material which has been contemplated for use by pupils. It seems to me that curriculum development might be taking a line which suggests conditioning of a kind I cannot support.*

The CEO was reported to have said at a public meeting that he would not have the Project in local schools. The anecdote raises a fundamental issue: that of the role of the LEA in innovation. Is it *in loco parentis* to teachers? Our assumption was that the role of the LEA in dissemination was as communicator or facilitator, not promoter or censor.

When LEAs do involve themselves in a programme of communication and support for innovation, how are they seen? There are, almost inevitably, problems of authority. What aspires to be a balanced presentation of a curriculum possibility to teacher judgement is construed as an LEA recommendation or mandate. If things go wrong in the classroom the LEA is likely to be seen as the impediment, usually because there are difficulties of resources and manpower; the dominant image of the LEA is as guardian of the purse. What return on investment do LEAs expect or do teachers feel obliged to produce? Success? There was some evidence during the pilot phase of the Project that experimental teachers experiencing difficulty in the classroom felt guilty. It was perhaps easier to open up the problems to the Project team than to the LEA contact. LEAs had not yet built a response role for themselves; they were more often seen as sponsors than as partners in an enterprise.

We have discussed, among ourselves, a programme which would explore the problems and possibilities of working towards a new role, in curriculum

* There were some interesting antecedents. In July 1969, two schools in this small county borough, after receiving publicity about the Project from Heinemann, expressed interest. The LEA was sent the names of the schools on August 11. On August 14 the CEO wrote to us: 'I have not, as you anticipated, received any firm requests concerning courses from these two schools.' On October 24 the head of one school wrote: 'I have approached my local authority about particulars for training in Exborough but I understand from the AEO that he has, as yet, no knowledge of this development of the Project.' On October 31 the gist of the letters was communicated to the CEO. He replied on November 12: 'As a result of your letter I have undertaken a somewhat closer examination of the papers we have received from you regarding the topic. I am rather intrigued by the sub-topics which you quoted on *War* for discussion by 14- to 16-year-olds of average and below average ability. Before I discuss with my heads whether we should send any members of staff to be "inducted" as "trainers", I should be very interested to see personally some specimen copies of the collection, especially the one on *War*.'

There was no further correspondence. The letter in the journal was clearly the result of the CEO's examination of the material.

development work, for LEA and research teams. Collins,[9] at the conference mentioned on p. 39, saw the potential of this new conception:

> In the long run the adviser can only hope to be successful in his role as a change-agent in so far as he works *with* schools towards solutions that the schools themselves are seeking, each party having equal power to influence the thinking of the other. This can be a slow process. (p. 15)

Traditionally, teachers have been accustomed to validate themselves to LEA inspectors and to project research teams; in the new regime, LEA and research teams would have the task of validating their work to teachers.

The nomination of a Project contact within the LEA staff

Where there is no structure for LEA response to nationally developed projects, then responsibility for different projects is likely to be allocated to – or claimed by – different individuals.

It appears that it is not particular tasks or responsibilities that give power to individuals in the LEA system; rather that tasks derive importance from the status of the individuals whose responsibility they become. The Humanities Project is not in a traditional subject area. Responsibility for it is not therefore likely to go consistently to the same kind of person – there is no extensive network of humanities advisers. Nor, if it were to go consistently to Curriculum Development Officers, would there be great expectations of uniformity of response since the appointment has been made in only a minority of authorities; moreover, where appointments have been made, the role of the officer is interpreted in a variety of ways and power is not consistent from area to area.

The local dissemination of a project will differ according to the status of its nominated contact, and according to his interest. For one inspector a project can be an additional and even potentially embarrassing responsibility; for another, it can be a major interest and learning experience:[9]

> Because the humanities field is my own field, I involved myself closely with what these two schools were doing and worked in the classroom with the two teachers. (p. 15)

In another LEA, the commitment of the Project contact was very different:

> I met a man who had initial responsibility for HCP in the area. He had established a pilot school but was obviously far from sympathetic

> to the Project in its pure form. His major interest was in resource centres and the value of HCP materials as a component part of the local resource centre. (report by AD, Project team, 1971)

The latter quotation exposes another issue: that of providing opportunities for the LEA contacts to become familiar with the Project and to assess its implications for local schools. Of course, how much the LEA contact needs to know will depend on the role he chooses to play. Whatever the role, we felt it important that the LEA should have realistic expectations about the difficulties of innovation.

As long as LEA officers have no common grounding in the study and evaluation of innovative classrooms and institutions, then mobility is likely to be disadvantageous to dissemination. The new adviser or inspector may have little inclination to pick up the threads of a complex project that he has not been involved with in his former position; the departing adviser or inspector may not have an opportunity, in a more senior appointment, to maintain his interest in a particular project. We found that LEAs rarely saw the need to inform the Project team that the HCP contact had left the authority. New contacts that we did hear about were invited to open days and training courses.

Our feeling was that mobility among experienced humanities teachers is likely to be helpful to the dissemination of a project. (Even if they move away from teaching and become teachers' centre leaders, inspectors, in-service-training tutors, the project can provide a *speciality* which builds a personal identity and marks out a distinctive area of concern.) On the other hand, mobility among LEA contacts is likely to be detrimental to the dissemination of a project. Where dissemination rests on persons rather than on structures, continuity is likely to be more at risk.

The identification of a local training team

LEAs are partly conditioned in their response to innovation by the overall conception of a national dissemination programme. The early HCP training courses were specifically for LEA teams; the LEA contact had the task of finding and briefing a group of people who would work together at a central training course and take responsibility for the planning of local meetings and courses. The task of identification and briefing seemed generally more difficult than we had anticipated. Part of the difficulty was that there was no single subject seam to explore for recruitment; humanities spans a number of disciplines.

It seemed that LEAs, in general, did not know their teachers and were insensitive to the importance of briefing, or perhaps they were uncertain of its substance in that the local policy for dissemination was not firmly formulated. Some LEA contacts commented, retrospectively, on the problem of identification of personnel:

> One significant function the adviser has is as 'talent-spotter.' (p. 15)[9] . . . suitable 'second-tier' leadership, i.e. people (may be centre leaders, but should be key teachers, heads or assistants) who can guide local groups in centres or schools in continuing dialogue about the Project, its materials, resources, operation in schools, examinations, etc. The $64 000 question is, of course, where do you find these? How do they emerge? (notes from an LEA adviser, 1971)

We do not know what procedures LEAs adopted for gathering their teams: some LEA contacts probably passed the recruitment responsibility to the heads of their most reliable or reputable schools; others, it seemed, accepted volunteers to the course and did not disclose to teachers the possibility of a local training role. There were exceptions: in one area, excellent screening resulted in the LEA being represented at the first dissemination conference by a teacher who subsequently built and sustained an experimental approach to the Project in her school, in the locality and even in the region. She was somewhat surprised to be known to the local authority. She wrote:

> I do not know exactly why the LEA suggested that I should attend the York course, for I had done nothing before concerning adult courses, nor given talks in public, nor worked closely with authority officials. I suspect they relied upon my interest in curriculum development, which was apparent in school and in the views I expressed at a local study group set up by the LEA and attended on occasions by advisers. (report by a teacher, 1973)

One obstacle to effective talent-spotting seems to be the subject territories of LEA officers and the administrative load that they carry. If local authority staff were to affect different kinds of specialism (evaluation, study of classrooms, and so on) then they might be better able, as a group, to make more informed judgements about drawing on the teacher potential in their area.

Local evaluation of curriculum development work

We observed, between 1969 and 1973, an increasing interest in, and need for, competence in evaluation at local level. This need in part grew out of a particular situation: that of the pilot school. The pilot school challenges local interpretation and understanding. There were areas which had a pilot school during the Project's experimental phase (1968–70) and there were areas where the LEA had designated a pilot school for the dissemination phase (from 1970). We are concerned, at the moment, with the latter. It was difficult for LEAs to know what to make of the pilot experience, and therefore to justify the tactic. Perhaps they hoped the experiment would be an outstanding success.

The early trust shown by the Schools Council and the Nuffield Foundation in the power of examples of 'good practice' has been a block to the development of a more realistic and more professional approach to the dissemination of ideas. What was missing was a respect for context, and a sensitivity towards the ways people may react to other people's success. Belief in the generative power of good practice dies hard, understandably so; its easy efficacy must appeal to the overworked educationists on LEA and project staffs. We increasingly found, however, that teachers we worked with were sceptical and realistic, ambitious of understanding, conscious of the significance of themselves and their schools as variables in the learning context. It is the problems, not the quick successes, that reward study. The myth of the dissemination of good practice has almost had its day. Present interest is in the dissemination of understanding, and this implies the development of skill in the evaluation of particular learning situations.

Areas with no local dissemination programme

This chapter has been largely concerned with the issues that surround positive decisions about participation. We consider briefly here the position of the school wanting to embark on a demanding project but located in an area where there is no LEA policy for local dissemination, whether by judgement or by default. The survival of the experiment will depend largely on two things: first, the quality of the central (or regional) induction course attended by the teachers (in terms of its capacity to set realistic expectations of progress) or the quality of the teachers' reading and interpretation of any project handbook; second, the interest and understanding of the head. The absence of external local support may serve to strengthen the internal support system. And there may be links outside the locality that provide lifelines for the innovating teachers – a project bulletin, a regional meeting of project teachers, videotapes (for hire) of work in project classrooms.

We have not had resources to study the development of the Humanities Curriculum Project in a school that is geographically isolated or is the only institution in the area involved in the Project, but in the section on self-training in Chapter VI there is an account by a teacher who embarked on the Project on his own in an army school on the Continent.

V. Communication

In the dissemination of the Humanities Project, the communication task was made difficult in four ways:

a by the language of the Project itself;
b by a tendency for decision-makers and practitioners, in responding to a project, to accept the authority of persons rather than of evidence;
c by the possibility of distortion;
d by the absence in most local authorities of a clear and public statement of policy.

The language of the Project

In the early days of dissemination we became aware of the problem of words and meanings and our perception of the problem has not changed. It was identified in an article by two members of the team:[10]

> The development team needs to give thought to the language of communication. A central team working closely together and with its experimental teachers will inevitably build up an in-group set of words and phrases which function as a relief map to the project's thinking. In time, as novel insights are more confidently identified, language hardens into an efficient in-group shorthand. Familiarity diminishes the expectation of misinterpretation, and either new phrases and new uses of old words will have to be carefully defined against present understandings, or simple longhand equivalents will need to be traced out. The inbred language of the early stages of experiment will not meet the needs of the diffusion of curriculum development. (p. 153)

Words are chameleon things, taking their colour from their contexts. In innovation we tend to promote half a dozen for special duty: these carry the insignia of the enterprise. The characteristic set of words in the Humanities Project was: neutrality (and sometimes, rather grandly, procedural neutrality); evidence; chairmanship; understanding; issues; agenda; premises; hypothesis.

In themselves the Project's key words are rather ordinary. Nevertheless, 'premise' and 'hypothesis' may imply a consciousness of intention and rigour of self-study that is alien to some classrooms. The words are apt but the associations threaten. 'Chairmanship' may signal to the outsider the tedium of committees; 'evidence' is too readily identified with facts and whatever is indisputable. 'Neutrality' is the most emotive word and it causes the most trouble; it is interpreted by opponents of the Project as emasculation of personality and moral leadership, and by the unenergetic but committed (and the energetic uncommitted) as a *laissez-faire*, feet-on-the-table casualness.

In a five-day course, and to some extent in a one-day meeting, participants can work through to understanding, but there is a second-stage communication problem, which teachers become aware of when they return to school after their reconnaissance trip to a training course: 'How do I tell the head what neutrality is in half an hour, *and* ask for half-classes?'

Influences on response: evidence or authority?

What do decision-makers need to know about a Project? It is this question that has shaped the work of the Humanities Project's evaluation team. The Project team itself was concerned with a different issue: the relative power of the source and content of the communication. House discusses this point in *The Politics of Educational Innovation*.[11] He is referring to models developed by Hagerstrand [12,13] to account for acceptance and resistance in innovation:

> Models I and II assumed that the stimulus for acceptance was information about the *properties* of the new phenomenon. Model III assumed that it was information about the acceptance of the innovation by certain persons that produced additional acceptances. In other words, one does not buy a radio when he hears about it; he buys it when he hears that his neighbors and friends have bought one. The focus then shifts from information about objects to information about persons. (p. 8)

If this is so, then it runs counter to the values of the Project as they inform its practice in dissemination as well as its practice in the classroom: the Project seeks to replace the authority of persons by the authority of evidence.

The possibility of distortion

House, exploring his image of innovation waves, writes about broadcasting, transmitters and receivers. His propositions have some relevance to the communication problems inherent in a 'training of teachers' strategy:

> There are many sources of messages, as there are many broadcasting stations. The messages are sometimes similar, sometimes disparate. As they traverse the social networks, however, the waves intermingle, sometimes in phase, reinforcing one another, and sometimes out of phase, conflicting with one another. The receiver picks up garbled messages, usually because several messages have been transmitted simultaneously, which must somehow be deciphered. Only under rare circumstances – a 'lab' school having direct contacts with inventors – are there any laser-pure messages.
>
> If one compares the original innovation with its implementation, it looks impure, more like a mongrelization of noise, because of the perversity of the receiver. But that is only because the sender sees just the pure light of his own message. The receiver, the teacher, sees a *mélange* of messages traveling to him over his own personal social networks. He integrates them, as he understands them, based on his own reference groups. In those rare cases where innovator and teachers work closely together the teacher's view may be very close to the inventor's, blocking other messages. As the teacher moves away from this closed situation, however, the demands of other social groups become increasingly strong in proportion to distance, both geographic and social. (p. 14)

As responsibility for communication is invested in points increasingly more remote from the centre, then it is likely that the communication will undergo change – a kind of Chinese curriculum whispers game; the content may be weakened or distorted, but – and this possibility is seldom acknowledged – it may be strengthened. Members of the Humanities Project team have had little experience of teaching the Project in schools; teachers who have worked with the Project in the classroom for three years or more and who become involved in local training courses can, we believe, provide the basis for a richer discussion. Their understanding is being extended by day-to-day experience; ours only by the vicarious experience of teacher reports and evaluation studies.

Uncertainty about LEA policy

The Project chose to work through LEAs as the main organizing agency in dissemination. We did not, initially, write direct to schools. Instead, we sent all relevant information to LEAs on the assumption that they had a responsibility for determining and controlling their communication moves.

The consistent weakness in LEA communication was the absence of straightforward statements of intention. Schools wanted to know where they stood. They needed to know whether the LEA was intending to organize local training courses, whether the initiative for participation lay with the schools or with the LEA officers, who the LEA contact for the Project was, whether fuller information about the Project was available locally, whether Project materials were held in the area and could be inspected, whether the LEA was offering any financial support to schools, whether there was any limit to the number of schools that could both participate and secure material support.

A few local authorities were exemplary in the public articulation of policy. The following extracts are from circulars about the Project signed by a Chief Education Officer in a county area. Letter A was sent to schools; letter B to teachers' centres.

Letter A, June 1970

> Teachers who wish to embark on this work will do well to undertake some form of preparation. A conference arranged at Brighton * by the Schools Council early in April was attended by a number of teachers, all of whom were from Anonshire, with a view to equipping themselves to help in the induction of fellow teachers in their own areas who may wish to undertake such preparation. It is hoped that groups of such teachers will be formed at certain teachers' centres in the county and that the groups will have the help, as chairmen, of those who attended the Brighton conference, or of others who are known to have knowledge and experience of the Humanities Curriculum Project. The proposed arrangements have now been agreed by the Committee.
>
> This letter is intended for your information rather than as an invitation. The Committee does not wish to exercise any persuasion on

* The first three dissemination courses were held at the Universities of Leicester, York and Sussex (near Brighton).

heads of schools to embark on Humanities Curriculum Project type of work. The meeting on 8 November 1969 (within the county) established clearly that in the view of the Humanities Curriculum Project team, the school will need to accept certain conditions as to the deployment of staff, and the size and stability of class, timetabling, accommodation and expenditure, if success in the undertaking is to be made possible. It may well be that heads wishing to make a start will decide to defer it until September 1971 or until some intermediate point during the school year 1970/71. You will be aware, however, that experience in the pilot schools suggests that success does not always come at once and that often at least a term can pass before the materials and methods begin to show educationally valuable results.

In regard to expenditure I am glad to be able to say that the Committee are able to offer schools limited grants over and above their normal allowances – such additional sums to be used towards the purchase of materials and equipment, the hire of films, the organization of visits, etc., related specifically to curriculum development of the type envisaged. The amount per school of such additional financial help must of course depend, among other factors, on the number of suitable schools wishing to participate.

If your decision is to proceed with preparations for a start in Humanities Curriculum Project work, whether in September this year or September 1971, I hope you will feel ready to co-operate with the warden or secretary of the appropriate teachers' centre in his arrangements for meetings there. You will be aware that at least two teachers will need to be engaged in Humanities Curriculum Project work in a particular school and it is clearly of importance that all who are to be so engaged should attend the meetings. I am writing to the wardens or secretaries of the teachers' centres proposed as meeting places for groups of interested teachers and I am inviting them to take the initiative in forming such groups.

I enclose a tabulated summary of the centres proposed, their wardens or correspondents, and the teachers who are being invited to undertake the chairmanship of the groups.

Letter B, June 1970

The Committee trust that you will, as indicated in the letter, be able to take early steps towards the formation of a study group whose

> main purpose would be the preparation of its members, during the remainder of the present term, to undertake work of Stenhouse type in their own schools. Provided the size of the group did not grow too large there would, of course, be no objection to the participation of other teachers who from general interest wish to learn something of Humanities Curriculum Project ideas. . . . The attached list shows (*a*) the chairman proposed for your centre and (*b*) the schools in your area known to have shown an interest in the Humanities Curriculum Project materials.
>
> Sets of an induction pack of materials, together with copies of a tape-recording of children in discussion, both prepared by the HCP team, are being obtained here and will be made available to groups formed at teachers' centres. . . .
>
> It is probable that from four to six meetings of the group will suffice. No doubt the precise number needed will become clear as the work progresses and can be determined later by the group and chairman together. . . .
>
> For teachers at schools that in fact embark on Humanities Curriculum Project work next autumn term, continuing meetings will, without doubt, be of importance in fostering success of the work. The timing of such meetings may be left for later decisions but it seems probable that they might start after, say, a half-term's interval and continue at three- or four-weekly intervals. At such meetings, tape-recordings of actual discussion sessions in schools will be of value.
>
> I feel sure that you will be ready to collaborate in this undertaking and I wish every success to you and the group that you are able to form.

It was not a teacher from this authority who wrote to us and said: 'All the information the LEA could supply me with was your address.'

After our first round of open days and training courses we became so disheartened by the general lack of effective communication within LEAs that we opened up the problem with the Schools Council. A Joint Secretary wrote the following paragraph in a letter to a widely known Director of Education:

> What causes us concern is the much simpler question summed up by the fact that Stenhouse would assert that about half the people on the York training course had no idea why they had been sent at all

and some, indeed, did not even know they were going on a course connected with the Humanities Curriculum Project. They had not been shown the letters to Chief Education Officers explaining the rationale for the course and had no idea of the nature of the diffusion process – limited though it is – of which they were a part. . . . I am convinced . . . that there are in many authorities serious gaps in internal channels of communication. There is evidence of this from other projects in relation to other courses also. (May 1970)

VI. Training

Within the Humanities Curriculum Project, training was mainly organized nationally (the central courses run by the Project team) and locally. The local courses might bring together teachers from a number of schools or they might be located within and organized by one school for members of its own staff ('within-school training'). In each training setting two issues are important: the problem of authority and the nature of training.

The problem of authority

In a nationally developed project, responses to authority are likely to affect decision-making in many areas where it is important to sustain teachers' initiative and independence of judgement. Extreme responses to authority may produce a polarization: a curriculum cult or a curriculum rebellion, faith in central professionalism or faith in the relevance of the home-grown curriculum.

Authority may derive from the inherent status of the sponsoring agency, from the acquired status of the project team and from the delegated status, or experience, of the local training team. The three groups fit the pattern of the analysis of power given in *Twelfth Night*: some are born great (the funding agency), some achieve greatness (the project team), and some have greatness thrust upon them (the local trainers).

Projects funded by a reputable institution carry a prestige which can reduce the likelihood of personal, critical scrutiny by clients. Joint sponsorship is generally dealt with by pinning colours on one or other of the sponsors: the HCP is commonly referred to as either 'The Nuffield Humanities Project' or 'The Schools Council Humanities Project'. A still more telling index of authority is the labelling of a project through its director – 'The Stenhouse Project'. Dissemination should seek to avoid generating a commitment to projects, persons and institutions, and foster instead a commitment to the ideas that they represent.

The authority of the central development team is most marked in direct confrontation with teachers during the dissemination phase of a national curriculum project. Members of the team tend to have no substantial teaching experience of the project in schools and yet there is an expectation that they can make easy generalizations and propose strategies that will guarantee successful implementation in all situations. Teachers are compelled to shelter behind authority partly because innovation is disturbing and partly because there is little understanding of the role of research workers in education. The task of a research and development team is to provide materials and ideas to support teachers in their exploration of new approaches, and to provide experimental data that will feed their judgement in decisions about adoption and organization or in dilemmas of classroom practice. It is not the role of a central team – nor of a funding agency or local training team – to make mandatory statements about what the curriculum should include or how features of the curriculum should be handled. The peculiar authority of a central team should lie in the research standards that discipline its work.

To summarize, the authority of a funding agency may diminish teacher responsibility for making choices, on intrinsic criteria, among alternative curricula; the authority of a central curriculum team may induce dependence over details of strategy, and this dependence can lead both to a disregard of contextual differences in the implementation of innovation and to an expectation of easy success. In dissemination programmes where some responsibility for communication and support is assumed locally (probably by a group of people who either have long experience of the work or have been trained by a central team) the same pattern of dependence and expectation can be replicated.

Authority is dysfunctional when it diminishes the play of personal judgement. But it can be helpful if it challenges heads and LEA officials to give thought to the organizational conditions for a project's introduction. Teachers who have come to central training courses without a background of understanding in their schools or of support structures in their locality have been pessimistic about persuading heads that half-classes are essential for HCP, that innovating teachers need time for reflection and planning, that storage of materials needs to be designed in relation to classroom practice. Authority is put to good use if it secures conditions favourable for the experimental work.

The problem of authority may not be peculiar to centrally developed curriculum projects. It may be as difficult for teachers to resist the locally generated and locally managed curriculum projects as it is for them to resist the power of the pedigree national projects:

> There is now a good deal of evidence that locally based innovations are sometimes seen by their prospective clients as more, rather than

less, potentially threatening than nationally based ones. Except for the relatively few teachers in any area who are directly involved, the products are just as 'external' as those developed by a central project team; but because, in theory, any teacher in the area *could* have participated in the development work (as we *could* all of us participate in local government), the results are in an insidious way less easy to dismiss. A kind of schizophrenia may be built up in which teachers feel trapped by the democratic apparatus of locally based innovation, but resent it and ultimately reject it nonetheless.*

The nature of training

Training is a bad word. Its associations build resistances. It seems to imply a relationship between experts and novices and to be about the transmission of skills. The intention at Project training courses is to build understanding, and thereby help local authorities and heads make informed decisions about implementation, and teachers make soundly based responses in the classroom. The pre-condition of 'sound response' is an attitude that recognizes two things. First, that the context of innovation is different from LEA to LEA and from school to school; teachers must therefore be prepared to experiment in the particular circumstances of their own classrooms – to set up and test hypotheses, to modify strategies, to interpret effects. In this sense, a training course is one stage in a process of self-development. Second, that innovation is generally a painful process and that projects will not work overnight miracles. Teachers are unlikely to survive in innovation unless they emerge from a training course feeling keen, determined – and pessimistic.

Training can release the independence of teachers; the untrained teacher can be trapped in a lonely set of misunderstandings and misapprehensions. The importance of training was confirmed by the results of the evaluation team's measurement programme. These showed trends in desirable directions in areas generally thought to be important for students: vocabulary scores, self-image and attitude towards school. On these three dimensions, the changes were significant only in schools where teachers had been trained or had long experience of the Project.

* R. A. Becher, in an unpublished paper on the dissemination and implementation of educational innovation, given at the annual meeting of the British Association for the Advancement of Science, Swansea, 1971.

Central training courses

SUMMARY OF INFORMATION

Timing and numbers
1970 – 3 courses, approx. 100 at each; 1971 – 3 courses, approx. 40 at each; 1972 – 3 courses, approx. 50 at each.

Length
All five-day residential.

Membership
The early courses were for teams of trainers; after 1970, participants came as individuals or as school teams rather than as LEA teams. From 1972, there have been more participants from abroad.

Staff
From 1971, experienced HCP teachers were invited to join the staff team. In 1973, the five-strong staff team for the Easter conference included only one member of the Project's original central team. In 1975, the staff team consisted entirely of experienced HCP teachers.

THE STRUCTURE AND CONTENT OF COURSES

Over the past three years, the changes in the training-course programme have been partly a response to the shortcomings of each preceding course and partly a response to the changing needs of the participants. Throughout, the main working group of the conference has been the small group.

Latterly the conferences have been presented more as an enquiry into the Project, itself a controversial issue, much as students in schools would enquire into one of the eight HCP themes. Evidence takes the form of videotapes of work in classrooms, statements and articles by teachers and students, case-studies of schools and LEAs, the measurement results, the Project handbook and materials, the experience of participants.

Each year, as our understanding of the Project grows, it seems more difficult to contain the course within five days. For financial reasons we decided not to extend the length of the course. The fee (at Spring 1973) of £29 covered accommodation, subsistence, tutorial fees and some copies of Project articles.

Some issues and events have demanded a continual rethinking:

- **a** the philosophy of the Project, particularly the procedural neutrality of the chairman and the concept of controversiality;
- **b** the practical experience of chairmanship;
- **c** the examination of materials and the way materials relate to the issues under consideration;
- **d** non-discussion aspects (or modes) of enquiry;
- **e** inter-group communication and competition.

The philosophy of the Project

At the first series of training courses, the Project was new to all the participants. Several small-group sessions were required for participants to explore and question the Project handbook and understand (though not necessarily accept) the Project's premises, aim, and essentially experimental approach. Misunderstandings arose and had to be worked through. Sometimes antipathies emerged as understanding increased: participants may not have known enough about the Project before enrolling for the course to realize that they were temperamentally or in principle opposed to it.

In time, the premises of the Project became more widely known and the number of sessions given to direct exploration of the Project's values and central thesis was reduced. We hoped that understanding would be deepened through the critical study of the experiences of the conference itself. But familiarity with the Project's principles did not necessarily imply understanding. We realized that it was still important for groups to grapple for some time with the premises of the Project.

The concept of neutrality commonly generates misunderstandings. It is often interpreted as extreme recessiveness: people assume that traditional chairman moves (questioning, summarizing, seeking clarification) are denied them if they are being neutral. The confusion is between substantive neutrality and procedural neutrality. A chairman can be neutral in respect to the issue under discussion while being active in the exercise of his responsibility for relevance and standards in the enquiry. He needs, however, to be alert to the possibility that moves which are ostensibly procedural may in fact have substantive implications: for example, he could unconsciously be seeking clarification on only those views to which he was personally sympathetic instead of ensuring that all the views represented were accessible to the group.

A major anxiety is that neutrality is a de-humanizing force. It needs to be seen instead as a protective device adopted *because* the teacher is strongly committed on most controversial value issues, and because these value issues are being explored in a situation where merit and not authority is the criterion by which ideas are judged and where, given the traditional authority of teachers, any expression of the chairman's views could well lead to partial perceptions of the area under discussion and premature closure on issues. Neutrality is not a way of life; it is a criterion by which a teacher can choose to judge his performance. It is a variable in a learning strategy and its potential is what Humanities Project teachers are exploring.

Another common area of misunderstanding is the nature of controversiality. The Project's learning strategy has evolved from the recognition that the issues thrown up by the eight areas of enquiry are likely to be controversial. On the surface, the notion of controversiality presents no problems. The danger signal is the statement that begins: 'But society takes the view that . . .' Such protestations may well mean that on certain deeply felt issues the teacher is not prepared to be neutral and his justification is that 'society' supports his point of view. To put it more blatantly:

> On matters controversial
> My mind is very fine
> I always see two points of view
> The one that's wrong and mine.

If 'society' is at one in its perception of, or position on, an issue, then the issue is no longer controversial. In some cases, the notion of controversiality can be refined by considering both how widespread and intense is the concern that an issue can generate: for instance the issue of women's rights is different in these respects from the issue of the authorship of Shakespeare's plays.

There are, of course, some values which are axiomatic in our system and the Project is explicit in its respect for these values: tolerance, rationality, imaginativeness. Similarly, the values of life and freedom are not, in our society, in dispute. It is therefore not consistent with these values to posit as controversial such issues as 'Is war good or bad?' Controversiality would work at different levels; for instance, 'Are there any circumstances under which war could be justified?'

Controversiality seems often to be just under the surface of things. One of the problems that has emerged in the Project is the difficulty of locating the worth-while threads of controversy in any area of lively interest.

Another is the distinction between value issues and issues which can be settled by empirical evidence. The Project assumed that phrases such as 'value judgement' and 'value issue', which derive from philosophical discourse, need no explanation or exploration. Training courses have shown the folly of that assumption.

Practical experience of chairmanship

In all courses there have been opportunities for participants to chair discussion, using Project materials, and to take part in an analysis of the discussion. These sessions are generally found to be valuable. There are, however, several organizational dilemmas. Should all members of the group (maximum 13) have chairing experience? If not, should there be self-selection or a drawing of lots? How can the analyses of discussion be structured to protect participants from destructive criticism? How do chairmen new to the Project familiarize themselves with materials? How far can members of the Project staff chair sessions without establishing exclusive 'models' of chairmanship?

It is important that participants see that effective and neutral chairing is often active in its interventions and that it can be accomplished in a variety of styles. A pattern of active chairing may need to be set by the group tutor while videotape recordings of classroom discussions may give evidence of the relationship between procedural neutrality and personal styles.

It is difficult to find a way through the problem of familiarization with materials which does not constrain the scope of the enquiry. Participant chairmen may have to work, acknowledging the artificiality, on pre-determined issues with pre-selected samples of materials. Even at this level, the experience is capable of raising a range of problems in the areas of relevance and control, pace and participation, the nature of evidence and the management of materials.

Our approach, recently, has been to try to involve all members of a group in either a chairing or an evaluatory role. It is helpful for the staff member to chair the opening discussion of an enquiry and to be subject to formal critical observation by one or two members of the group; a pattern of acceptance of feedback is then established. It is usually essential to suggest particular focal points for the evaluators: for instance, the selection and timing of the introduction of evidence; breaches of neutrality; patterns of interaction. Evaluators sometimes find it useful to record the discussions, to interview chairman and group independently on certain problematic sequences, and then to play back the tape to the whole group in order to see whether perceptions of what is happening are in accord.

Examination of materials and the relationship of materials to issues
If teachers are to regard the published materials as 'core' or 'starter' collections which they will extend and up-date, then it seems important that they understand the principles of coverage, depth and balance by which the materials were selected. Latterly, three or four sessions at a training course have been given to the detailed study of one collection of materials. Participants, working in twos or threes, select issues and examine how far the materials would support the exploration of those issues. The exercise raises questions of coverage and priorities, of balance and bias. It also makes possible some classification of issues and the kinds of exploration that different kinds of issue require. The findings are generally reviewed in a plenary session so that some general picture of the strengths and limitations of a collection may emerge. It is important that teachers are encouraged to take a critical view of the materials.

Non-discussion modes of enquiry
The pattern of early training courses reflected the Project's assumption that what would be novel in the Project was the style of discussion and that other modes of reflection and enquiry – interviewing, survey work, hearing and questioning speakers, reading, personal projects, role-play and simulation, painting, writing, making or composing – were traditionally part of a teacher's repertoire and therefore needed little examination at the training course. This imbalance has meant that some have perceived the Project as being based exclusively on discussion. Time is needed at training courses to examine such questions as the relationship between neutrality and non-discussion activities; the locus of responsibility for initiating and organizing non-discussion work; the relationship between group discussion and the insights acquired through group or individual research and expressive activities; the ratio of non-discussion activity to discussion; the organizational implications of non-discussion activities; the confidence of teachers in handling activities that lie outside the range of their subject-teaching experience (drama, for instance); the question of standards (where students in Humanities lessons paint, write or act in order to explore particular issues, how and by whom are standards – in art, literature, drama – mediated, and is attention to these standards important?).

Inter-group communication and competition

A training course which works mainly in parallel small groups reflects to some extent the patterns of curiosity and anxiety and the problems of communication and understanding that are identifiable in a school where there are several Project groups and one team of teachers. The parallel might be extended to a teachers' centre meeting where teachers from different schools meet to understand, explore and learn from each other's experiences. There seems to be a need at training courses to provide opportunities for formal exchange of ideas and experience, and for a recognition that groups will inevitably proceed at different paces and in different styles, and will often move through phases of loyalty and hostility to their chairman as they learn to be independent and yet to make the most of the resources – skills and materials – that the chairman has to offer. It is important, therefore, to balance plenary with small-group sessions and to maintain, despite the pressures of coverage, timetabled but unspecified sessions which can be programmed by the groups or used to defuse the conference as a whole if inter-group tensions build up. The 1973 programme (see Appendix C) is weak in this last respect. The 1971 and 1972 courses timetabled group-confrontation sessions where groups came together to share experiences of the course and to satisfy their curiosity about procedures in other groups. We called these our 'bleeding sessions'. They were difficult for members and for staff, and other pressures seem to have squeezed them out of the timetable. We are fairly enthusiastic about their revival.

Local training courses

In contemplating a 'training of trainers' approach to dissemination we had underestimated the importance to trainers of classroom experience. We envisaged that training would give the local team sufficient understanding of what was significant in the practice of the Project to enable them to help local teachers mount appropriately organized and monitored experiments. In many areas, however, the local training course was postponed until the teachers who had attended the central training course had tried out the Project in their schools. The security of the trainers seemed to be closely tied to the resource of classroom experience.

We have had neither time nor personnel to evaluate on a broad spectrum the effectiveness of local courses. The details that we have of programmes, comments and follow-up work are in no way representative; they are merely examples that we came by through the courtesy of local organizers who were concerned to keep the central team in touch with what was happening (as, in the interests of accumulating evidence, we had requested). They have been selected to show a range of courses (residential and non-residential, long and short). The programmes (reproduced in Appendix C) are of courses that took place between 1970 and 1973; some carry critical reports from the organizers and participants. The comments that follow illuminate what proved to be the central issues for local training: structure and organization; the involvement of heads; problems of leadership, coverage and focus; attitudes and anxieties.

Structure, organization and membership

> . . . for those schools seriously considering using the Project, I propose next term to try to run a full induction course, either to run parallel with the starting of the Project in schools, or as a preliminary to its starting in January or September 1972. The form of this course is under discussion and I shall be very glad to have your comments on the two broad possibilities, which are: (*a*) a series of about eight sessions, on a given evening each week, of an hour and a half; (*b*) a shorter intensive course for two whole days, Friday and Saturday, nearer the beginning of term.

> The course needed to be more centrally placed as X school (the conference site) is on the southern border of the city. The time was not particularly convenient as it was difficult for some intending participants to leave their own schools early. Some forty people attended the first two meetings . . . but there was a noticeable drop in attendance for the last two meetings. Bearing this in mind, it probably would have been better to have held a one- or two-day course at the teachers' centre or training college, which are more centrally placed . . . possibly a member of the central team in attendance at future meetings could prove an added 'draw'.

> Three days was too short. A residential course would have been better but we have no facilities for this yet.

> There's no doubt about it that when our dissemination was residential it was much more satisfactory, I think, in a way. There was a great feeling of a group developing. And I think this business of being at it in the bar afterwards and when you get up in the morning at breakfast – this is, I think, very important.

It was very clear to us that the members of staff there were convinced of the total ignorance of their headmasters with regard to the Project . . . they felt that their heads just simply did not understand the implications of the method, and the possible repercussions that this might have on discipline issues and, well, every decision that is taken in the school.

Since the introduction of a Humanities course in a school will raise problems of staffing, timetabling, accommodation, and finance, I feel that before the training programme begins it would be advisable to hold a preliminary meeting for heads.

Three of us will be involved with planning and supervising the three-day course. It is essential that the course is attended by the head-teachers of the schools concerned, as well as the teachers who will be directly responsible for the introduction and use of materials.

Leadership

They thought they would have liked to have more of the Project team at the beginning – I don't know whether this was to attack them or not. They thought the enthusiasm-value of having people from the Centre * at the conference would be good. One or two people were very nice about the way I introduced the Project. 'Yes,' they said, 'but we would like it . . .' (they didn't say straight from the horse's mouth), '. . . we would like it straight from Lawrence Stenhouse himself. We would like to have had Miss Rudduck or Lawrence Stenhouse, both Jean and Lawrence together, at our conference because we feel that, no matter how well you did it, Mr X [the local inspector], and of course you did it terribly well, we would have liked to hear it directly from the Centre.' And I saw their point. To some extent teachers here are at the mercy of how I interpret the Project. But there are lots of safeguards, both in the materials themselves and the, you know, the strong good sense of teachers. And also of course in the handbook and what's been said before. There was Mr Y [an experimental teacher] at the conference able to answer their questions. They felt afterwards very enthusiastic and one of them went up to Mr Y and said: 'I had doubts about the whole thing, but

* Centre for Applied Research in Education at the University of East Anglia, where the Project was based from October 1970.

when I saw you managing that discussion with those kids (on videotape), you know I really feel enthusiastic. I think I can do it and I am going to try.'

Attitudes and anxieties

The majority of people who came were, I am not quite sure of the right word, but certainly were suspicious of the method. They were very suspicious, particularly of this neutrality business.

There was a good deal of discussion of neutrality. They were worried about neutrality in the original choosing of the materials and about the balance of ideas represented in the materials. . . . They were worried about the confessional atmosphere that began to develop in some of their own chaired sessions when private evidence and experience was put forward and secrets were divulged about family life, and they wondered about this in terms of pupils – well-meaning teachers trampling over secret areas. They felt they weren't trained in group dynamics, nor were they expert at group therapy, and they felt that some of this was quite close to that area at times.

Our major problem has been firstly impatience from the teachers when we refused to give answers to specific questions. We tended to throw the questions back to the group. Secondly, a natural desire: they wanted to talk straight away about organization, and the specific organization within their school and the local authority. They gradually understood that these points would come up in later sessions and that we wouldn't deal with them just then. Thirdly, there was a certain amount of inhibition because the LEA man popped in and out of the sessions.

Faint indications of good-humoured despair.

Coverage and focus

It was a pity that I hadn't got with me samples of follow-up work, the sort of thing that might have been used or developed by the children in a CSE Humanities course.

X asked if it would be possible to have a recording of a pupil discussion. Y said that they would have appreciated a panel of people, who had actually used the Project on the shop floor, to query at the end of the course.

> . . . a session on examinations and examining at which I spoke and gave the school's impression of how to try and use the Project for a Mode III CSE. This was very valuable indeed because all the schools had this examination phobia and wanted to know whether it (examining) could be done. It's the sort of topic I would suggest is always considered at one of these meetings.

Within-school training

A few LEAs sponsored the attendance at a central training course of one teacher from each interested school. In some areas these trained teachers formed the nucleus staff for a local training course; in others, teachers had the task of inducting colleagues in their own school without the external support of a course. The need for induction in order to achieve a coherent working basis was not always recognized:

> In Mrs W's school three teachers are involved; even she does not know whether one man has been trained or not and he doesn't seem to have any communication with her. The group said that if he was small, thin and dark then he had shown up at one of the local support meetings. Innovation apparently rests very lightly in the minds of teachers in this school. (report by JR, Project team, 1971)

Within-school training probably needs to be formalized. Where a nucleus HCP team is already established and induction is for one or two new members only, one approach is an extended programme of observation of the experienced teachers at work – almost an apprenticeship. A more difficult situation is where one or two centrally trained but inexperienced teachers have the task of inducting other teachers in order to build an HCP team to staff the experiment. We can document only one strategy here. In this school, the projected size of the HCP team was ten; five had been recently trained. The induction for the other five was a two-day meeting held on a Saturday and the following Monday (the head released the team from their timetable commitments on the Monday). On the first day, thirteen students from the local college of education were invited and the team leader and his trained colleagues chaired HCP discussions. He chose outside students because he did not want expectations of the Project among his own students to be contaminated by any events at the introductory session. His colleagues watched and analysed his chairing. On the Monday, sixth-formers came from two local schools. This time the five new teachers chaired and were in their turn analysed. A sense of local responsibility – this school was an LEA pilot school in the first year of dissemination – may have strengthened the school's readiness to arrive at organizational compromises for the sake of the induction course.

It seems that every form of potentially worth-while within-school training will make some demands on school organization: unplanned training, which readily lapses into casual, coffee-break chat, cannot be expected to yield understanding, nor would such an informal approach promise adequate support to teachers embarking on the experiment. The need for rigour of approach is still more acute when the process is one of self-training.

Self-training

We have data from one teacher who persevered for a year with the self-training approach outlined in the Project handbook and was then given support to attend a training course. The extracts are from an interview that he gave at the end of the training course. It may be that his sense of isolation compelled a disciplined approach (he was in a British Army school abroad):

> I decided that the best way to introduce it, having read the handbook was, because I'm teaching RE, to abandon RE in the fourth and fifth year, to introduce a social studies programme for one year, to get them used to discussion and project work, and then to begin with the Project itself.
>
> I didn't even introduce the Humanities Curriculum Project. It merely cropped up. There was something topical in a newspaper, the group wanted to discuss it, and it just so happened that it coincided with *The Family*.
>
> I first of all read the handbook through at one sitting. Having read it, I then thought that perhaps it wouldn't be a bad idea to go through and pick out the main points, like chairing and other activities. (I eliminated in the beginning other activities that I thought I was bad at – the things I couldn't do with my groups because of the type of person I am.) I had to decide just how purist I was going to be as a chairman. Whether I was going to stick to the letter as far as being the neutral chairman, allow the silences, not to be corrective in any sort of punitive sense. And so, having read the handbook through

a second time, making my points, I thought about them. Then I read the important passages again, the ones that I decided were to be my main objectives; chairing obviously was the most difficult of them.

There was no chance of my coming to an open day or going on a training course for quite some time, so the only thing I could do was to see how it worked and then to make judgements. I thought that if I tried to adapt before I'd actually tried the method then I would fall down.

I felt isolated. I used the tape-recorder. I used to play it at home on my own machine, and listen to it on the headphones, criticizing myself. I felt that I wasn't being critical enough in that really I had nobody else to discuss it with and nothing else to compare it with. I would have valued other people's advice on the things I was doing which were cropping up over and over again; I didn't seem to be able to correct myself. The discussion would often go round in circles and I began to ask myself when I should feed in fresh evidence. This was tremendously important. In the early stages I was very amateurish. I wasn't really learning from my own mistakes. I did feel that I was making progress, but it was a long process, a very long process, of learning to recognize when the time was right to feed in evidence, or when to call in a child to discussion if he had been sitting silent for a long time. . . .

There were eleven months when it was hard going. I didn't feel they were responding. If I had somebody else in the school that I could have talked to about it I think I might have broken through.

I have got more idea now (as a result of attending the training course) how to organize material, how to play out the role of the chairman, also had to collect ideas about the way in which an issue can be introduced, and ways of gathering issues. . . .

I've been able to talk to people about these problems and certainly been able to see what other lines people are working on. 'Other activities' is something that has worried me, not only because I haven't had the time but because I feel that my capabilities are limited. I've been very wary about introducing drama, but now I'd try it whereas before I wouldn't. . . .

You saw some videotapes where the discussion was going on in just the same way as your own discussion goes, and you saw on certain occasions your own mistakes; it hit you in the eye. It was almost ten times worse than when it actually happens to you. When you are in that situation you make a judgement; you think it was the right thing to do. I have learned that there is a time when you have just got to judge how the discussion is going. Another thing is to see how, on the videotapes, the chairman deals with the quiet person, deals with the rowdy person, and deals with minorities. One coloured child we saw was brought in to the discussion and made his contribution; it wasn't very much but at least he spoke his point of view.

I think the most important step that I must take is to find colleagues in the school who want to be taught in. Not to have them selected for me, but to find colleagues who are willing to be taught in, who are interested, who want to know more about it. To teach them in and then to allow them to make the decision whether or not they want to do the Project. (recorded by J R, Project team, 1972)

VII. Support

Support is crucial to innovation and the responsibilities for support, in the dissemination of the Humanities Project within the British system, are shared by the LEAs, the heads of schools and the Project team. It would be misleading to think of support merely in terms of 'after-care', although this aspect is the one generally under-represented in the management of innovation. Support has the dual implication of fostering opportunity for innovation and providing a maintenance or after-care service.

Support and the LEAs

THE INVESTMENT OF MONEY

> Alone schools cannot introduce and maintain major, expensive projects from normal capitation. (LEA adviser, 1971)

Innovation needs LEA money, but in 1970 LEAs were generally experiencing straitened financial circumstances. Lack of funds was the most commonly cited reason for an authority's declining to involve itself in the dissemination of the Humanities Project.

Financial investment is largely seen in terms of purchase of materials, whereas it might be more appropriate for decision-makers to think in terms of buying potential for teacher development.

There are, in fact, many calls on LEA money in an innovation such as the HCP: for resources – printed materials, film purchase and hire, additional equipment such as portable tape-recorders, ancillary staff to help achieve half-classes of students; for training – fees for central courses,* travel to local support meetings and to central courses, payment to teachers serving as local trainers, hire of videotapes, local conference costs. From the

* At central training courses there was generally some resentment at the varying contributions made by LEAs (maximum 100 per cent) to the costs of attendance – especially if teachers both had to make a contribution out of their own pockets *and* saw the course as preparing them to take a local training responsibility for the authority. LEAs also varied considerably in their conventions for paying teachers who worked in their own time on local training courses.

school's point of view, the money that buys resources buys time; it increases slack in the system and without slack, innovation will barely get a foothold and will certainly not survive.

As more opportunities for involvement in curriculum innovation present themselves, priorities have to be determined; in the words of an LEA inspector, 'the test will come as other Schools Council projects stake their claim'. But in many areas there seemed to be no coherent policy for curriculum development which would provide criteria for planned expenditure. Nor was there always a contingency fund that would enable an LEA to make a spontaneous response to opportunities that emerged too late for forward budgeting – not everyone was prepared for the curriculum deluge. In the absence of policy, the power of individuals is paramount. The amount of LEA money invested in the Humanities Project was in some cases an index of the status and commitment of the LEA Project contact. It was not merely a case of how much the LEA contact could commandeer but how much he was prepared to seek!

We detected some financial anomalies as LEAs confronted dissemination. Two stood out:

1 Some LEAs took a cautious plunge: these were the circumspect, setting up their own well-supported pilot school and holding off the involvement of other schools (the constraint was generally, one suspects, imposed by financial rather than educational concerns). The other interested schools had to wait and watch, but it was often uncertain whether a similar financial float would be available to them if and when they took up the Project. LEAs appeared to be budgeting for failure rather than for expansion.

2 Some LEAs, following what seemed to be a prodigal policy, sent a stream of teachers to the centrally organized training courses (at a cost, for residential places, of over £20 per head, plus travel) whereas by establishing a local training system and using their already experienced teachers as trainers they could have channelled the money into consolidation strategies – buying films, establishing support meetings and so on. But it seemed that the budgetary heads for teacher development and curriculum development were quite separately controlled.

Where LEAs were forced into frugal investment they either supported one school, the local pilot school, or they bought a central cache of materials so that interested schools could work to a rota system of borrowing materials until they could make their own purchases. The disadvantages of the scheme are obvious, but there are advantages: schools can take materials 'on spec' and if they choose to make an investment, they can select from the available themes on the basis of experience rather than hearsay. And schools that come late to take up the Project are still able to benefit from the authority's initial investment.

THE INVESTMENT OF PERSONNEL

Support is not just a matter of money; it is also a matter of understanding:

> If an LEA were hostile to the Project and were responsible for diffusing it locally there could be disasters, and also of course if the LEA happens to use an inspector or adviser or administrator who didn't understand the Project very well, this could be bad. (LEA inspector interviewed by JR, for evaluation team, 1971)

There were many signs of uncertainty in the LEAs – about the nature of the Project, about the implications of the Project's dissemination strategy, and about the hazards and pressures of innovation in general. Members of the local training team seemed often to have been carelessly chosen: teams happened rather than were planned for, and they were frequently unbriefed about any possible role in dissemination; they in their turn became uncertain of the limits of their responsibility and the territory in which they could exercise initiative.

One way for the LEA to gain understanding of the Project was for the Project contact to attend a central training course as a member of the local team. The Project had strongly recommended this move. Nevertheless, there were many teams left unsupported. On two occasions this lack of support was functional in that the teacher teams became militant on their return and demanded support from their LEAs. The more aggressive of the two prepared the following statement in Spring 1970. It represents the teachers' view of the support that the LEA needed to provide if the experiment in curriculum development were to be seriously tackled (the LEA did, in fact, respond sympathetically):

Report and recommendations of training team

> **1** *Co-ordinator*
>
> As no LEA officer, nor Curriculum Development Officer, attended the course it was not possible to nominate a co-ordinator.

Of the three possibilities: (*a*) an LEA officer, (*b*) Curriculum Development Officer, (*c*) member of the training team, it is recommended that one of the latter be appointed because of their specialist knowledge in this field.

Please note this must be done immediately and the information sent to the Project's director.

2 *Prerequisites for instituting the project in Exborough*

a Finance

This must be made available to the trial schools in the first instance and other schools as they develop courses. £80 per year is advised for films and an estimated £400 per school for the packs.

b Suitable staff

i. Project leaders must be able to pick their teams, who *must* attend the training courses (see below).

ii. Sufficient staff must be available for the teaching groups to consist of 12–15 members. The staffing ratio of the schools, therefore, must be adjusted.

c Courses

(Please see Humanities Curriculum Project paper A* on the timing and nature of courses.)

The courses will operate initially in the trial schools where study groups will be set up. These should: (i) meet a half day per week over a ten-week period; (ii) meet in conjunction with the other trial schools.

d The training team

i. The co-ordinator. Time must be allocated for him to: organize training sessions; communicate and visit the schools concerned; visit the Education Office, teachers' centre, college of education and central Project team for consultation.

ii. The team. They will be responsible for training teachers in the authority and will help diffuse the Project in the classroom. Therefore they must have time to: observe, train and encourage teachers in the classroom, which from September 1970 will involve visiting schools; set up study/experimental training groups.

* See p. 29.

Without full LEA support for the team and Project, the experiment will fail.

3 *Equipment*
a Collection of materials at the teachers' centre, especially a library of film extracts.

b Humanities rooms to be established in each school with the following provisions:

i. filing cabinets for the packs of materials, i.e. adequate storage;
ii. tape-recorders, film/slide projectors and overhead projectors;
iii. videotape facilities.

c Each school to have its own collection of packs of materials.

d Materials from the Project's central team to be purchased (perhaps for the teachers' centre) for training purposes:

i. published collections;
ii. handbooks;
iii. training tapes, both audio and video.

4 *Remuneration of trainers*
Considerable work, outside school hours, will be necessary on the part of trainers. Consideration should therefore be given to payment of the training team.

5 *Co-operation with colleges and departments of education*
They must be made aware that the Humanities Curriculum Project is operating in schools.

It would be appreciated if a meeting could be held immediately to discuss these matters with administrators, the Curriculum Development Officer, and the heads concerned. If the authority is to make this project operative in September, it is imperative that training commence immediately.

A few LEA contacts achieved a deeper understanding of the Project by working on the experiment in a school, alongside the teachers. It is interesting to speculate whether the classroom involvement of the LEA contact contributed significantly to the stability of the local team. We were not able to follow up systematically the dozen or so instances that we had on record.

Accounts of their own Project teaching by LEA officers suggest that the pay-off for this way of investing time may well be in terms of relationships with innovating teachers. LEA personnel are clearly not immune from the frustrations and disappointments that frequently dog the early days of innovation for teachers. A Senior Assistant Education Officer, the Project contact in a county borough, wrote to us in November 1971. He and two others, another LEA officer and a college lecturer, had, as a team, attended a central training course in 1970:

> Each Friday morning I take a group of fourth-year leavers using *People and Work*. There has been perfect co-operation from my colleagues in the school but I am struggling with this group. Only my faith in what you are trying to do keeps me going. I have reverted to more formal teaching in an effort to get to know the group better!

In a telephone call two weeks later he explained that a group in the school was going well with a teacher 'older, and much loved by the pupils'; he added that he thought 'the experience would be a good basis on which to discuss problems with local teachers.' A member of the Project central team (JR) commented, in a report of the discussion:

> He sees very clearly how difficult the work is and is now writing a paper on the raising of the school leaving age in which his experience of difficulty is to be reported. Today he is having a working lunch with Humanities teachers who have some problems to talk through.

We should like to have known at what cost to his other commitments does an LEA officer become deeply involved in one project. Experience showed that some officers could afford quite generous chunks of time for whatever they chose to observe or support closely. We do not know how best such time might be spent, whether in making individual visits to schools, in talking with innovating teachers about their work at group meetings, in maintaining the organizational superstructure for dissemination in the area, or in practising the project in the classroom.

In one very large LEA, understanding of the need for support in innovation was manifested in the creating of a special post. The authority had been involved in the pilot phase of the Project, and in the first two years of the locally organized dissemination programme teachers from almost 90 schools attended the training courses; not all, of course, subsequently embarked on the Project. Consolidation rather than expansion was needed and this meant a full-time post:

> Secondary Advisory Teacher – Humanities Curriculum Project. Applications are invited from experienced secondary teachers for secondment as an advisory teacher to work with the Inspectorate on collecting and disseminating information about the Humanities Curriculum Project in the authority's schools. Experience with the Project, interest in curriculum innovation and a commitment to in-service training are desirable qualifications. Duties will include visiting schools to record details of how the Project is being explored, helping to plan courses, assisting with preparations for videotape recordings and other means of dissemination, and generally enabling teachers to benefit from the experience of others. Secondment will be for two years and an allowance (£350 full time) will be paid in addition to existing salary. (advertisement in *Contact*, the ILEA house magazine)

LOCAL SUPPORT MEETINGS

Local support meetings, usually held at teachers' centres, are occasions when teams of teachers from schools in the area involved in the Project come together in discussion groups. The Project team recommended that such meetings be established for several reasons: in the absence of any national association of Humanities teachers they would ensure some continuing community of interest; from the teachers attending these meetings would come the personnel to staff any subsequent local induction courses; thoughtfully planned and handled, they would be some brake on the speed at which the Project would become another orthodoxy, with the experimentalism dropping out of the work. (This is inevitable and indeed desirable – teachers cannot perpetually work at innovation pitch – but it is advantageous that the potential of a project should be fully explored before there occurs a stage of institutionalization.)

The local support meetings were not without their problems. These were, in the main, problems of leadership, competition and purpose.

Leadership, at least in the early stages, generally fell to the teachers' centre wardens, who experienced some conflict over priorities and role (see Chapter VIII, p. 101). Sensitive leadership could be essential in some areas in order to manage the tensions arising from a confrontation between schools where the immediate contexts were so different that near failure was as likely in one as near success in another. It was important to contain competition by harnessing the differences in an exploratory, research-oriented approach. Teachers might hypothesize about the reasons for the varying impact of the Project, and study together the effects of any moves that the support group had proposed in response to the problems encountered. There was the associated difficulty of teachers describing experience in an honest and meaningful way so that the members of the support group could make a constructive response.

There were a host of other, mainly organizational, problems at support meetings. A research interest in the experiment requires some continuity of membership and regularity of meetings but these criteria were often hard to achieve. Teachers involved in innovation often seemed to be the busiest teachers and they had other commitments. Moreover, support meetings sometimes had to accommodate the experienced Project teachers and the inexperienced, the over-committed and the over-sceptical. And there was uncertainty about the kind of agenda that could sustain the meetings. If support groups have neither research interests nor practical tasks (such as gathering local materials as extensions to the published materials, developing a CSE syllabus, building a film library) then the meetings are likely to fold up after a while. Project support groups, if they are to have a worth-while life, must be capable of helping their members to function at the level of ideas – by formulating hypotheses and testing them in their classroom – and at a level of practical productivity.

One LEA contact, a remedial adviser based at the local teachers' centre, sent us a diary of the Project support group's meetings over a period of five months and this is reproduced in Appendix D.

SUPPORT WITHIN THE SCHOOL

The case for support is vividly put by the Project's evaluation officer, Barry MacDonald, in *People in Classrooms*: [14]

> Curriculum projects generally support their claims by offering a variety of endorsements from enthusiastic teachers and, even allowing for partial selection, it is hard to escape the conclusion that experiment lightens the teacher's psychological burden, that for the innovator in the classroom: 'every day is different and exciting . . .' When it comes, however, to full-blooded innovation involving the manipulation of major variables in a teaching/learning situation, then the fine line which separates an adventure from an ordeal becomes blurred.

> . . . The lot of the HCP teacher is not, in general, a happy one. It's not difficult to understand why this should be so. Every new curriculum provides a mixture of familiar and novel elements. Those who try them out derive support and comfort from the familiar while they explore and develop those aspects that are new to them. But the Humanities Project is largely a venture into the unknown without support. It is more than a modification of the teaching process; it is a fundamental reappraisal of the nature of the exercise, and as such it has implications for the whole of the secondary school, implications which are readily seen by those who are threatened by them. (p. 9)

And in the last issue of the Project's evaluation bulletin:

> HCP teachers know they've been in an innovation. They can show you their bruises.*

The case for support is perhaps rather floridly put. MacDonald calls for casualty units in an army field hospital, whereas what is in fact needed is thoughtful planning and realistic expectations.

The experience of the Project has revealed the crucial importance of the head in innovation. If the experiment is to be profitable, the head must regard himself as having an investment in it. Ideally, a project should be introduced as part of the school's policy for change or for sustaining change, and the organizational decisions should be made with the kind of care and understanding that policy effectively commands.

If the initiative for taking up a project comes from teachers, then they face the problem of manœuvring the head into a supportive position, and that implies a readiness to examine the project's potential for the particular context of a particular school. If the experiment is to be seen as a respectable concern of the school as a whole, then it will need to be given status. Status can be achieved in a number of ways: by the involvement of senior members of staff (perhaps the opinion-leaders in the school); by the involvement of a wide ability-range of students so that the work is not immured in the non-examination fourth-year classrooms; by the allocation of appropriate rooms and resources; by the trouble taken to win the interest of the community. One aspect of support for innovating teachers is, then, the security of being seen to be involved in an enterprise which is recognized as demanding but worthwhile.

* 'Innovation and incompetence', HCP *Evaluation Report,* No. 9, November 1972.

Another aspect is protection from petty criticism: a head will need to manage any tensions within his staff that the innovation engenders. Tensions often have their source in threat, resentment or envy: the innovating group of teachers may be released from school to attend training courses while other teachers have to mind their classes; the innovating teachers are given new resources; they are visited and interviewed by members of the project team or even by the local press; they may be involved in videotape recordings of the work in their classrooms; they are likely to have some moments of enviable enthusiasm and their students may actually say to other members of staff that they prefer the work of the project to the usual curriculum fare. Innovation can be tough on those who are not involved.

The extent to which a head meets the organizational pre-conditions set up by a project team is some index of the school's commitment to the experiment. Pre-conditions in the Humanities Project were half-classes of students, training for teachers, a timetabled period per week for the team to plan and to reflect on their experiences, rooms appropriate to small-group discussion, and the availability of a tape-recorder to each group when involved in discussion work. The third was the most rarely achieved, even in experimental schools, but the Project did not collapse for want of it; the team would generally meet in their own time. The first – the need for a maximum class-size of twenty – was much more a test case for dissemination. We found in the experimental schools, where commitment was generally rather strong, that heads were able to achieve half-classes if they tried. In dissemination, commitment by the head is generally more elusive and large classes, to judge from the number of complaints we listen to, have been one of the rocks on which the experiment has foundered. Our advice to teachers at training courses has been to refuse to embark on the Project unless half-classes can be managed. The fact that half-classes are not achieved could in itself suggest that the Project is held in low esteem in the school.

The head will face a range of organizational decisions about any innovation (as opposed to a piece of curriculum renewal), especially if the innovation is not in a traditional subject area of the curriculum. One set of problems concerned the staffing of the Humanities Project. Should the Head identify individuals who are interested, even if they come from different subject departments, and mould them into a team? Will this team constitute a new department or will the members' overriding loyalties be to their original department? Or will he locate the Project in an existing department (social studies, English, religious education, have been the most usual choices)? What are the promotional implications of a teacher involving himself for part of his time in what might be seen as a fringe activity? (There have been instances of teachers both losing and gaining promotion as a result of their involvement in the Project.) And there are other decisions to be made. Which students to involve, and how many? Should the experiment start small and rather quietly and be somewhat protected from scrutiny until it has something to say for itself (an approach adopted in one school where the head expected fairly strong resistance), or should it start large and publicly, with maximum involvement of staff, even in peripheral roles? How much time does the Project need and what length of session is appropriate? Where can time be found; should the Project replace a subject or should several subjects lose one or two periods a week to make time for it? (A risky practice if the pared-down subjects are offered in public examination and the Project is not!) What kind of room is conducive to adult discussion – the relaxed comfort of a common-room, the rather austere privilege of the Board of Governors' room, the upright chairs and blocked desks of an ordinary classroom? What are the pros and cons of submitting the students to a Mode III examination in the Project; is an examination necessary to command the respect of students and parents in the area? At what stage might parents be involved in the Project and in what ways: should they be invited to join discussion classes for an evening or a term? Should they be shown materials, even out of context? What financial allowance does the team need and, if humanities is not an official school department, where does the allowance (for visits, films, tape-recorders) come from? Are the resource materials adequate in supply and location so that unnecessary pressure on teachers (and distortion to the teaching strategy) can be avoided?

Our experience during the experimental phase suggested that there were some institutions that would be unlikely to provide adequate support for an experiment of this kind, particularly those that were undergoing substantial reorganization: *

> It seems that an experiment settles well in a school where teachers are confronting a problem and contemplating action. The experiment should extend the range of their strategies for dealing with the problem. However, where an internally conceived programme is

* These hypotheses are being tested in the dissemination phase by the evaluation team, who are preparing a report.

already well advanced, involvement in a national curriculum development project either produces bewilderment or results in an exploitation of elements of the national programme with no generalizable experimental data.

It is sometimes suggested that experiment is more likely to succeed against a background of stability rather than of flux. This may be so; it needs to be looked at carefully. Many schools in England are in the process of reorganization (this generally implies that a secondary school is becoming comprehensive). The new system which emerges may retain or even reinforce the existing values, but it may represent a change of values. Where the hierarchy is likely to be reshaped through reorganization, and where teachers are anxious about their future, the tendency may be to demonstrate solidarity with the status quo and not to undertake the risks of innovation – unless the values of that innovation are ones towards which the school is seen to be moving. (pp. 150–1) [10]

Support and the Project team

The range of services provided by the central team (including communication, training and support) is shown in Table 2 (no distinction has been made between the Project team and the evaluation team).

There is no place on the list of services in Table 2 for one important but nebulous feature of the support programme: the attempt to build a climate appropriate to research and innovation in schools, one which would be characterized by a realistic attitude to the difficulties of curriculum change, which would condone experimentation and accept failure as a professional hazard and source of further insight, which would not seek easy generalizations but concentrate on understanding the impact of innovation in particular circumstances.

Nor does Table 2 include one abortive attempt at national support, and two contributions to the strengthening of regional support services. First, the abortion. We attempted in 1973 to launch a magazine from the Centre for Applied Research in Education. This was intended to carry Project news as well as articles about other projects located at the Centre. We were optimistic in our expectations of subscribers and commissioned a fairly large and attractive format. We needed about one thousand subscriptions to make a marginal profit; the fifteen hundred or so people who had accepted the Project's evaluation bulletin when it was free were not, it seemed,

Table 2 Support services provided by central Project team

Type of service	*1970–1972*	*1972 onwards* [a]
Information	open days; lists of LEA contacts; lists of HCP speakers; pamphlets and articles; samples of trial materials	open days;[b] articles, pamphlets and publication lists
Training	central training courses (9)	central training courses (1 or 2 a year)
Personal contact	HCP teacher on six-month secondment, visiting schools; case-study of particular schools and LEAs; occasional team participation in local or regional HCP events	occasional participation by former members of Project and evaluation teams in local or regional HCP events
Audio-visual materials (videotapes of HCP in the classroom)	videotape hire system, with related support material	videotape hire system, with related support material[c]

[a] Some continuity after the end of the Project was made possible by two events: first, four members of the original Project team remained together to staff the new Centre for Applied Research in Education at the University of East Anglia; secondly, the Nuffield Foundation put its quarter share of the royalties from the sales of materials into a trust fund (the Continuation Fund) which would underwrite training and help sustain some support functions. The Schools Council later gave money for part-time secretarial assistance 1973–6.
[b] Ceased in 1973.
[c] Service suspended in 1973 owing to damage to tapes; resumed in 1975.

prepared to pay £1·20 a year for three copies of the new magazine. Our subscriptions crept up to three hundred. We withdrew and the Nuffield Continuation Fund covered the losses.

There were two rather more successful ventures. We gave some stimulus (ideas and £25 floats) to the setting up of regional associations of HCP teachers.* And we set up discussions in two areas (where there was little

* At December 1973, three had been set up: one in London (see Appendix D), one in Newcastle and one in Manchester.

Project activity organized by local authorities) for the establishing of regional centres; these centres, both based on colleges of education, would organize training courses, regionally or nationally, and would provide information and support regionally. The intention was that they would ultimately accept a brief that went beyond the Humanities Project to include other work in the humanities area.

The first blueprint for regional centres was sketched early in 1972 but the time was not ripe for the ideas to be taken up. The blueprint included the following passages:

1 In the Project's pattern of diffusion, LEAs are the key units of training, and the scheme is dependent on their responsiveness, resources, organizational strengths. There is tremendous variation. For us, the weak points thrown up by our pattern of diffusion include:

lack of considered experience of the diffusion of innovation;

uncertainty about the identification, role, powers and accountability of the official LEA 'contacts' with the Project;

unreliability of communication systems within the Education Committees, and between the committees and their schools and centres;

absence of any firm and generally acceptable basis of co-operation between authorities and colleges;

unevenness in the rate of growth of teachers' centres;

unevenness in the siting of teachers' centres within an authority in relation to the spread of schools; variation in the resources and role-definitions of teachers' centres; variation in (and uncertainty about) the definition of responsibility and initiative of leaders in relation to LEA curriculum development policy;

general unawareness of the importance of the preliminary stages of innovation: communication and organization (in particular, inattention to the role of the head and to the need for discussion-time for innovating teachers).

2 A regional structure would make good some of the deficiencies outlined above. It would be a guarantee of continuing opportunities for training and support, would maximize the resources of an area, and provide the security (especially in the inevitable disturbance of innovation which works in new subject areas) of group activity and reliable communication channels. It would survive the dispersal of the Project team at the end of its funding.

3 Its role:

Training courses and conferences
to organize training courses for local leaders (wardens, LEA contacts, team leaders from schools or colleges);

to help leaders plan local programmes;

to organize introductory meetings for heads and LEA officers;

to organize annual meetings for teachers working on the Project.

Communication of information
details of central and local meetings;

names of participating schools and their team leaders;

data on films, supplementary materials, relevant talks or broadcast programmes;

progress in such areas as examinations.

Services
to make possible an on-the-spot inspection of materials;

to exemplify indexing systems;

to put VT [videotape] facilities at the disposal of interested groups;

to provide advanced or specialized reprographic services;

to explore the possibility of alternative channels of local film hire and use (and possibly, later, of using CCTV [closed-circuit television] or local radio programmes). (internal paper, JR, Project team, spring 1972)

The brief was too ambiguous and too specific to the Humanities Project but the germ of its ideas was taken up in 1972–3 by the Schools Council Working Party on Dissemination,[15] and Humanities Centres were set up at Bishop Lonsdale College of Education in 1974 and at Berkshire and Northumberland Colleges of Education in 1975.

The major dilemma for the Project in establishing a fairly substantial support system was to find the balance between central activities which stimulated and serviced local and regional activity and those which stifled independent initiatives. Given the almost total lack of experience in LEAs in assuming responsibility for dissemination, the Project's concern for independence was too demanding. It forced people to plunge in at the deep end of dissemination, and, as one might expect, some swam and some drowned.

A case for support

A teacher, on his own initiative, had attended a Project training course in 1970. In his county borough there were no plans for local dissemination. Within the next few months, the man took up an appointment as adviser in the same area. He decided to gain some teaching experience of the Project before attempting to establish a local dissemination programme. He was not given any official responsibility for this move by the LEA; he was following his own interest. He contacted a comprehensive school that he knew well and it was agreed that a head of department would be inducted by the adviser and that two parallel groups of fourth-year leavers would work on the Project. In practice things turned out rather differently.

In this area there was no LEA backing for the adviser's initiative; the initiative was not high-powered (in the sense that it came from a newly appointed man who was formerly a local teacher). Nor was there in the area a group of energetically interested teachers to push for induction and support. The classroom experiment was treated by the host school more as a piece of self-indulgence on the part of the adviser than as a serious attempt at curriculum innovation. Against such a background the individual engages in a hopeless struggle; the slender foundation of a dissemination structure that the adviser tried to build in the school collapsed around him.

> So this was arranged and I thought that I was going to be working with this man, the head of department. In fact, a couple of weeks later, he said, 'You will, in fact, be working with another member of my department.' But I knew him, too, and he was a well-established member of staff, so I said, 'Fine', and then I tried to lay down a few requirements and said that I thought that this group or groups should be made up with volunteers, and since the head made it clear that only Newsom pupils could be considered, we had to draw them from that group. I said, 'I will have to leave the selection of the groups to you because I am not there, but I think you must have people that can read, you know; otherwise I leave the formation of the groups to you.' . . . When I got to the school I found that, in fact, the groups had not been arranged – they hadn't got round to producing the groups - so they didn't have a list of names to give to me, even though I had asked for this weeks before, and they had assured me that it was all in hand. Then I went to see the teacher concerned (the teacher whom I thought I was going to be working with). When I got to his

room, he was in the process of weeding out a group. I said, 'I'm going to be working with you', and he said, 'I didn't think I was going to be *working* with you; I thought you were going to be relieving my numbers.' So then I explained to him about the Project and he said he wasn't really interested in the Project anyway.

So there I was. I was in the room, the kids were there. They were sorted out, since my arrival at the school, into a group and they were waiting expectantly; they had been told that something was going to happen. I didn't think they looked particularly happy but I thought, 'Well, in this case I have just got to deal with this one group. Perhaps if it works reasonably well the teachers who are already there might take an interest.'

I explained to the pupils what the Project was for. I explained to them that, in fact, no one in Extown had done anything like it before, and that therefore a lot of people were interested to see how they got on. I tried to make them feel that they were doing something important, something worthwhile. I explained to them about the methodology of the Project and got them to think about rules for discussion, and they agreed to these.

Then I dealt with the problem of the chairman's role and explained that I would be adopting certain attitudes, and that there would be a reason for this. Then, the next week, we started to look at the pack and I gave them some of the pictorial materials and said, 'Just look at these for twenty minutes and try to jot down what sort of things come into your mind, what you think about in connection with war when you see these photographs.' They did this, and they mentioned a number of issues.

Then they started to get unco-operative, just little things. At first they started to snigger and poke one another, things like that. I had already pointed out that we would tape-record things and that we would play them back and discuss them, and so on. There were quite a lot of these youngsters, about eighteen or nineteen. They were really being extremely unco-operative and resentful, so I decided that we would not get anywhere; they were trying to push me towards authoritarian behaviour, and so I just said, 'Look, we will stop the whole thing and I want to talk to you, because there is something that is bothering you, and I am not quite sure what it is, but it's preventing any of us from working. I want to find out what's wrong.'

After a few sarcastic remarks, one of them said, 'There is nothing wrong with us except that we don't want to be here', and so I said, 'Why not?' They said, 'This isn't very interesting is it?' But I didn't feel that that was really the problem. I said, 'Well, that may be the case but I am sure there is more to this. I am sure that, for some reason, you are being antagonistic towards me and I'd like you to tell me why.' They said, 'Well, we didn't want to be in this group, anyway, and we are only in this group because he doesn't like us and wanted to get rid of us.' So I just said, 'Who's he?', and they said, 'The teacher that you got us from.' So I said, 'Well I thought you were all volunteers', and they said, 'No, we are not.'

So then I said, 'Is there more to it than that?' They said, 'Well, we don't want to be in this lot, because you are only doing things like talking about things and the others are going on visits.' And so I said, 'How do you know that we are only going to talk about things; we haven't had a chance to develop things. I told you that we would have to develop things as we went along and that if a visit seems necessary we will arrange a visit, and so on.' They said, 'But the others are going off and doing what they like – going off on visits and things. Because we are with you, we can't go.'

Now that put me in a difficult position because I knew, in fact, the remainder of the group were going on visits, but I also knew that they hadn't gone on visits before this disruptive element had been taken out of the larger group and, in fact, the teacher had said to me, 'Now that you are taking those, I can do something worth while and interesting with the others. But I wouldn't do it if they were in with them as well, because I can't trust them.' So even though I knew that, I couldn't say to them, 'Look, even if you were back with the others, you wouldn't be going on visits. The only reason they're going is because you're not there.' . . .

So I just said that in fact organization was quite complicated, but if it was only visits which were worrying them, I thought that the opportunity of visits would emerge from the work that we were doing. They asked me what kind of visits and, you know, being put on the spot like that, I just mentioned one or two things that came into my head – a possible visit to a museum, and so on – and they just didn't like this idea at all.

> They said, 'No, we want to do useful things, like seeing factories, and things like that.' So I was trying to see whether, in fact, we could salvage anything from the wreck, but it seemed to me, after further discussion, that there was really nothing we could do. They had just decided that they didn't want anything to do with this project. They had pre-judged it. So I said, 'Well, there is only one thing that can be done, really. I am going to try and get you re-integrated into another group, to do the sort of things that you want to do.'

The first group dispersed and the adviser began again with a second group of thirteen volunteers.

> The second group was doing quite well, but as I said, absenteeism was one problem. The other one was that we were getting on towards Easter then, and I said something about next term, and then I realized that only two of the thirteen would be there – they were all Easter leavers – and so, really, there was no point in my coming in as an outsider in this way. So I sent copies of my report to the head and other interested staff and I said that it had been a failure, and I explained why the first group was a failure, in my opinion. I said that the second group was something of a success, but that it really should have been planned at least a term in advance, that had the group been started in September 1970 they might well have done something very useful. But I said that really I could not say that the Project was a failure because I just didn't feel that the Project, as outlined in the handbook, had even been given a chance. So I said, 'I can only say, in the strongest terms, that if you seriously want to do this, you should think about sending somebody else on the training course. You should really look carefully in the handbook, look at the snags and look at the organizational difficulties.'
>
> The head wrote back and said, 'Thank you very much for your report. I have passed the other copies on to the other teachers and I know it will help them when deciding what to do with the material that we have available.' (from interview by JR, Project team, 1971) *

* A shorter version appeared in HCP *Evaluation Report*, No. 3, September 1971.

VIII. Influences and agencies

In a complex, densely contoured, decentralized system, can dissemination be effective if effort is concentrated on particular areas? If the aim of dissemination is to get ideas into the bloodstream of the system, how many veins have to be injected?

The Humanities Project team made a decision to work through local education authorities. What did this decision mean for other possible dissemination agencies and for other sectors of the system? What influences, beyond the control of the Project team, shaped the pattern and pace of response to the dissemination of HCP?

There were a number of agencies alternative or additional to the LEAs: the Project's pilot schools; teacher's centres; colleges, institutes and departments of education; Her Majesty's Inspectorate; Schools Council field officers; and the Project's publisher. The following questions were relevant.

> Was there a role for these groups in the dissemination of the Project?
>
> Would the Project need to define roles for them and take initiatives in involving them, or would they work out their own roles and sphere of activity?
>
> Could, or would, these groups become involved in ways that were supportive to the dissemination strategy adopted by the Project, or would there be tensions and opposition?

Major influences on the dissemination of the Project included: the evaluation programme; other projects in the humanities area; journals and the press; and the public examination system. We asked ourselves the following questions.

> In what ways would these elements shape response to the Project?
>
> Were they likely to be positive influences (positive in the sense of contributing to an understanding of the Project rather than to quantifiable adoption)?
>
> Could the Project have harnessed these energies more effectively?

The pilot schools

In the early years of Nuffield- and Schools Council-sponsored curriculum development, the concept of the pilot school grew up (with the sophistications of pre-pilot and associate pilot schools). In other countries, a development school or, more commonly, an experimental school, is generally one with extraordinary facilities and resources which is located on or near a university campus and is used as the test-bed for new ideas. By contrast, pilot schools in this country are ordinary schools, usually nominated by local authorities in response to the sponsor's invitation to participate in the early, pre-public phase of a project's development. In the pilot phase of a project, methods are evolved and materials field-tested. The findings and insights of the pilot phase serve to define the content and style of the public phase.

There is a commonly held assumption that the pilot (or trial) schools are the natural cells for dissemination. The experience of the Humanities Curriculum Project suggests that the role of the pilot school in the dissemination of innovation is more complex than it is generally assumed to be.

The Nuffield/Schools Council model

The Humanities Curriculum Project inherited, through its feasibility study,[3] the now familiar blueprint: a pre-pilot, extended pilot and public phase. As Banks points out,[16] even the number of pilot schools had become traditional:

> Certain demands are made of pilot schools which are not made of other schools later in the project; for instance, that they should use the materials as the project team intends them to be used (not piecemeal or mixed up with other material). And, once committed, they must undertake to see the project through. They will also be asked to provide the project team with a good deal of information about their experience in using the materials, and to report on the results, good or bad, as they go along. From the team's point of view, there is obviously a limit to the number of schools from whom they can assimilate detailed information of this kind, and indeed there is a limit to the number of schools that they need to give the materials a valid testing. Thirty is generally regarded as ample for this purpose. (p. 252)

It was part of the tradition to give free materials to pilot schools – hence the emphasis on field-testing of resources. Another Schools Council spokesman, Philip Halsey, wrote this:

> As soon as drafts were ready, trials of the new materials in schools were organized; these resulted in improvements to the materials and enabled the project team to identify the kind of help or training teachers needed before they could successfully adopt the new materials.*

The pilot schools contributed to the public phase indirectly, through providing evidence for the revision of materials and criteria for the planning of a communication and induction programme. But a more direct role in dissemination was also perceived by Banks:

> The better distributed and thicker on the ground the pilot schools, the more expertise there will be in different parts of the country with which to prime the second wave of schools in the following year. Pilot schools, in other words, do have a role as demonstration units, their teachers have a role as demonstration teachers, if and when they can be spared to assume this function. (p. 252)

The assumption that all pilot schools can serve as demonstration units in dissemination is what we would question; the writer seems to ignore the possibility of failure.

The selection of pilot schools †

The director of the Humanities Project stripped the experimental design of its traditional pre-pilot and extended pilot phases, and applied for an extension of time for dissemination and evaluation. The prescription of thirty pilot schools, 'well distributed', was accepted. The Council wrote in June 1967 to all LEAs inviting co-operation in the pilot phase of the Project – a grand, democratic, and possibly rather foolish gesture. There were 165 LEAs and only 30 schools to be selected. To be fair, the extended pilot phase was generally used to mop up the excess of schools offered by

* From an unpublished working paper on the role of research and development projects in curriculum development. The paper was given at an international training seminar on curriculum development, arranged by the OECD's Centre for Educational Research and Innovation at Norwich in 1971.

† Criteria for the selection of the pilot schools will be examined in the evaluation team's main report on the Project, which is still in preparation. We are concerned here with the implications for dissemination of the general approach.

LEAs in the pilot phase. In May 1969, the Council sent another circular to LEAs, this time inviting participation in the public phase of the Project. The repercussions of these two moves were important.

About half the LEAs responded positively to the first circular. A final selection of 31 was made, largely by the Council's permanent staff but in consultation with the Project director. These 31 LEAs alone had offered a total of 108 schools and one Curriculum Development Centre. Negotiations foundered in four LEAs and a further three were brought forward. The final count was 29 LEAs with one pilot school each, and one LEA (the large Inner London authority) with three pilot schools. Many schools were passed over; many LEAs were passed over. We have no record of letters of explanation being sent to LEAs that were not selected for involvement in the pilot phase.

At the dissemination stage, two years later, there was evidence of this earlier rejection:

> My recollection is that three of our schools were interested in this Project but that none was accepted as a trial school. This is perhaps fortunate since I believe the cost comes to something like £200 [*sic*] per school. It means, however, that there does not seem to be much point in our sending representatives to the second series of training courses. (letter from Chief Education Officer, January 1970)

Other LEAs were also mindful of rejection:

> Two or three schools originally applied to join the scheme but they were not chosen. (October 1969)
>
> In October 1967 I nominated five schools that were keen to participate. (July 1969)

Some LEAs who had been passed over at the pilot phase were still prepared to examine the potential of the Project for their schools.

The 1969 circular went from the Council in much the same way as the 1967 circular had done, and there were signs of confusion. LEAs did not always see the distinctions between the pilot and the public phases. One distinction was that the Project controlled participation in the pilot phase whereas in the dissemination phase initiative and responsibility lay with the consumers. We received many letters asking 'permission' to participate or asking whether schools were 'acceptable' to the Project team.

The number and spread of pilot schools

A broad spread of pilot schools on a one-school-to-one-LEA basis minimizes the communication task in dissemination. At the same time it reduces the likelihood of schools being closely supported from the centre and of being easily brought together in mutual consultation groups. To have reduced the number of pilot schools in favour of a firmer – and more economical – support structure would have been a challenging decision. The Project was very difficult to realize in the classroom; problems of communication and organization were paramount. During the first pilot terms, only a handful of schools were making any significant breakthrough. The experiences of these schools had to be distilled and transmitted to the other pilot schools as hypotheses to be tested during the second year of the experiment. In a sense, our first dissemination experience came within the pilot phase itself. Had there been fewer pilot schools, we might not have had enough common evidence of breakthrough to enable us to formulate anything substantial to disseminate.

A matter of terminology

We use the term 'pilot school' and 'pilot phase' for convenience. The term was in fact avoided by the Project, largely on the grounds that it supported the notion of a centre–periphery model of innovation, where the periphery's task is to test the centre's product. Such a model decreases the creative initiative of the periphery and leads to a situation where if the pilot experience is uncomfortable – and innovation generally proves to be so – the teachers feel that *they* are on trial and not the Project, and that they are 'failing' the central team. We preferred to speak of 'experimental schools', signalling the fact that teachers were co-operating in the development of the Project and that their work was being co-ordinated by the central team. But the old word died hard. The overtones of the new word were not universally attractive. Witness a letter from the Chief Education Officer of an area with an 'experimental' school:

> I do, however, object to this school being described as an experimental one. It is not and never has been an experimental school. It is a normal school, but like all good schools it is willing to indulge in controlled experiment. (August 1968)

It has been our intention in dissemination to sustain the notion of experiment; every school taking up the Project should examine its potential, in context, with the curiosity and patience of a committed research worker.

In a sense, the pilot schools might helpfully have been called 'development' schools, and the dissemination schools, 'experimental'.

The relationship in time of the pilot and public phases

During the pilot period, we considered the role of our pilot schools in relation to dissemination with increasing curiosity and concern. There was no space between the end of the pilot phase and the start of the dissemination phase; in fact the two phases overlapped, with the result that the energies of the Project team were somewhat withdrawn from the pilot schools in order to lay the foundations of the dissemination programme – and it was impossible for the evaluation team to ensure that their studies of the experimental pilot experience in schools could feed decision-making in the dissemination phase. Had the team been less stretched in 1969 it might have done more to help the pilot schools and their LEAs prepare for and accept a role in dissemination.

The interpretation of experience and the authority of experience

If the experience of pilot schools is to be drawn on directly, in face-to-face encounters with interested teachers, then more understanding needs to be generated of the problems of transmitting experience and assessing the status of experience.

There were, it seemed, as many experiences of the Project as there were experimental schools; it was irresponsible to generalize, and yet easy generalizations were called for. Teachers at the early dissemination conferences challenged the team in much the same way as Project chairmen are sometimes challenged by their students: 'You're paid to tell us'.

We first became aware of the problems of insularity and authority at the 1970 dissemination conferences. We had urged LEAs with an experimental school to include their Project teachers in the team that attended the central training courses; we felt it was important that the experience of the experimental teachers was extended before the local induction courses took place. Not all LEAs were as perceptive as the local inspector who wrote this:

> We have one pilot school but no close contact with other authorities in which the Project materials have been tried out. To avoid the danger of insularity we shall certainly need support from the central team. (1970)

At the conferences we distributed the experienced Project teachers among the small groups that were the basic working unit of the conference.

We noted the readiness of the would-be innovators to regard the experience of the one teacher from the one school as somehow representing the likely experience of all teachers in all schools. There was no quick understanding of what Parker and Rubin [17] had learned:

> Field settings differ in so many ways. What goes well in one situation may fail miserably in another. (p. 52)

In risk-taking innovations, where it is comparatively easy to fail, what matters is to profit from failure by understanding it.

> The point, of course, is that it is not enough to know that something doesn't work; it is also necessary to know why it doesn't work and under what conditions it doesn't work. (pp. 52–3)

What, then, of dissemination in localities where the experience of innovating teachers was not, on the whole, a happy one? Of the thirty experimental LEAs, seven did not, as far as we know, involve themselves in formal local dissemination work. Of these, two were small county authorities where plans for the reorganization of secondary education were compelling attention and resources; there were some uncertainties about the continuity of the experiment in the new settings. In another authority, the one experimental teacher, who had made explicit her dissatisfaction at the lack of support for the experiment, left the area. In four others the experience of the Project had not been entirely satisfactory. In one of these, where the experimental school was the largest and most noted school in the county borough (one where the LEA Project contact had an almost founding-father interest), there were no plans for local dissemination. The LEAs of the other three schools booked places at the conferences and then withdrew. In each pilot school there had been organizational difficulties: in one there was a large team of Project teachers with internal divisions; the Project was timetabled for near-remedial students who had no chance of tackling much of the printed materials. In another, high-status teachers associated with the enforcement of discipline were involved; this seemed to make it difficult for students to accept the credibility of the chairman's role. In the third school, the head expected the Project to succeed; promotion of teachers was at stake in the prelude to reorganization, but the Project was unexamined work in an examination-oriented curriculum and community, and therefore a low-status enterprise.

The curious common event in these three LEAs was the withdrawal from dissemination after fairly strong expressions of initial interest. The phenomenon may be attributable in one case to the relatively tenuous relationship between the school and the LEA contact; in another, withdrawal followed an introductory meeting for local heads, where either the experimental team may have urged dismissal of the Project as a failure or the audience may have been unable to perceive the significance of the contextual variables in distinguishing between the potential of a Project for themselves and the reported experience of one school. In none of these areas has training or support for the Project subsequently played any formal part in the LEA's policy for development.

It seems that where there are schools whose initial experience of an innovation is seen as disappointing (rather than as realistic in terms of the constraints of the setting), then dissemination is unlikely to proceed.

The teachers and the schools

There are two obvious reasons why the pilot school may not unquestionably be the natural cell for dissemination. First, it is unrealistic to take for granted the pilot teachers' readiness to accept an active role in dissemination. Second, the status and image of the pilot school may adversely affect the readiness of local schools to learn from it.

The selection of pilot teachers may have been erratic. The work was not in a traditional subject area and criteria for selection, other than an interest in innovation and in handling social issues in the classroom, could not be deduced at the pilot stage. Some teachers may have found themselves in a two-year commitment, of some national prestige, that was not easy to duck out of. Where the pilot phase had been uncomfortable, teachers' defence mechanisms may have led them, in public, to embellish their experience or to blame the Project, with the result that communication was unlikely to be disciplined by the need for the speaker and listener to achieve understanding of the evidence available to them. Nor indeed would all teachers be competent to communicate at a level that went beyond anecdote. Dissemination is partly about generating procedures and principles for describing and interpreting experience.

The central team had to ask itself whether it had a responsibility to LEAs to advise them of the potential usefulness in local dissemination work of the pilot teachers in their area. To put it more bluntly, were we to give warnings about people whose understanding of the work seemed less than adequate for a local communication programme? We decided to keep silent and to leave the task of observation and selection of trainers to the LEAs.

At national level, the Project team could make its own selection of teachers for the dissemination programme. These teachers were mainly drawn on to work in the staff team at central training courses.* In 1970, however, we attempted to equip a number of teachers from different areas of the country to speak about the Project at local, regional and national meetings. Twenty teachers were invited, thirteen from the pilot schools and seven from 'early adopter' dissemination schools. This approach was not entirely successful and only a handful of the twenty were subsequently involved in public presentation of the Project. It may be that the move was premature; subsequently a different set of public speakers emerged, presumably by a process of natural selection.

There is a fundamental problem in identifying people who will contribute to a stable structure for the dissemination of an innovation. Parker and Rubin [17] highlight the problem of identification, especially during the period of the Project's greatest impact:

> When one seeks to launch a new idea in the school, illustratively, one is likely to encounter at the outset a contrived enthusiasm based as much upon boredom or discontent as upon the inherent worth of the idea. If it catches on, a number of additional recruits are likely to enter the fold, also on a somewhat fraudulent base. (p. 42)

Where a dissemination system rests entirely on persons then, if the passage is right, the tasks of identification and selection are all-important.

We became interested in the mobility of the 150 experimental teachers but did not have resources to trace their progress in order to find out how many of them remained in the pilot schools, or how many of those who had changed schools, or moved from schools to teachers' centre and local authority posts, were still involved with the Project in some way.

If the selection of pilot teachers has implications for dissemination, so has the identification of the pilot schools themselves. Local response to the experience of a pilot school is likely to be affected by the image of that school. On what criteria do local authorities nominate a pilot school? We have no coherent data but we can speculate on the basis of piecemeal evidence. A school may be selected because it is regarded as laggard in innovation; if it is seen as an outsider, then teachers from other schools may be suspicious of submitting to its leadership. Or a school may be

* One teacher from an experimental school joined the Project for six months, visiting schools and local HCP meetings and working on one of the collections of materials.

selected because it is likely to do well for the Project, and it may be so much the apple of the LEA's eye that its leadership will be resented. And yet what matters is whether the experience of the pilot school can be presented honestly and can be interpreted in the light of its particular context.

In summary, the questions that appear, retrospectively, to be important are these.

What are the implications for dissemination of:

1 the selection procedure for pilot schools?
2 working with *x* number of pilot schools?
3 having a national spread of schools as opposed to a cluster around the project's home base?

What is the role of a pilot school in relation to dissemination:

1 in its area?
2 in the country as a whole?

What are the difficulties in dissemination for an LEA:

1 which has a pilot school?
2 which has no pilot school?

The pilot school may not necessarily be the natural cell for the dissemination of the Project. What is at stake is:

1 competence in presenting and interpreting unique experience;

   unrealistic expectations of success and uncertainty about the respectability of failure.

2 a readiness to be swayed by the authority of experience;

   a tendency to seek the security of easy generalization.

3 the basis for selection of the pilot school; its image locally;

   the mobility of personnel involved in the pilot experience and their sense of contract.

4 the size of the local authority and the efficiency of its formal and informal communication system;

   the personal investment in the experiment of the LEA Project contact and the closeness of his relationship with the pilot school.

Teachers' centres

Teachers' centres were not regarded by us as an alternative dissemination agency to the LEAs but as an extension: we tended to look on them as one of the resources within the control of the LEAs. The teachers' centres played an important part in the dissemination of the Project. Even as the centres themselves varied in their location, status, finances, amenities, staffing and interpretation of role, so did the contribution they made to dissemination.

Centre leaders were sometimes nominated by the LEAs as Project contact; in such cases they were likely to be a hybrid: half leader, half adviser, and therefore having more power. They may have been included in the local team that attended the central training course. In large country areas with a network of centres the leaders might exclusively constitute the local dissemination team.

The centre itself can fulfil a range of functions for the Project. It can be an information centre. If it holds Project materials it can contribute to local decision-making in a fuller sense: no specimen sets of material were available from our publisher and it was not easy for teachers to scrutinize materials without a minimum outlay of about £14 (the price of one teacher's set for one theme). But if centres are able to offer this kind of information, inspection, and even loan, service for all nationally or regionally developed projects, the expenditure would be prohibitive. By what criteria would a leader decide to stock materials for one project rather than another?

The most usual function of the centre is as a location for in-service training. In small county boroughs, the centre may serve all interested schools; in larger areas, several centres may simultaneously offer induction courses to satellite schools. In some areas the leader is closely involved in these courses; in others he merely provides space and facilities.

The centres may also be the setting for Project support meetings. Sometimes, however, teachers prefer to meet at each of the innovating schools in turn, better to understand, through the evidence of the actual environment, the kinds of problem that are being highlighted by the experiment.

Some centres may offer teachers practical and financial support in the purchase or hire of films and in the extension of the collections of materials. One leader cleared copyright on all local papers and invited teachers to select articles for a single-copy archive; he would then print copies of any item in the archive that teachers wanted to use in the classroom. He also negotiated terms for a three-year loan of films which Project teachers thought were relevant to the exploration of a number of controversial issues likely to be raised in the Humanities enquiry.

In a minority of areas, the centre has provided accommodation for Project groups from schools where there were no rooms available or appropriate for discussion work.

The involvement of teachers' centres in the dissemination of the Humanities Curriculum Project has thrown up a number of issues that relate to the status, competence and commitment of the centre leaders. We were often aware of the limited power of the leaders: they were generally unable to take initiatives that had financial implications and their activities were sometimes inhibited by problems of status. The problems of status became apparent in encounters with local heads and teachers. For instance, where schools involved in the Project were inappropriately organized for the experiment, centre leaders seemed unable to make forcible recommendations to heads about the conditions of innovation. If the leader was formerly an assistant teacher in the locality, his relationship with heads might be understandably ambiguous; if he was formerly a head, his dealings with other heads might be uncertain; if he was formerly a primary teacher then he might struggle to win the confidence of secondary teachers. Jack Walton[18] sums up some aspects of the problem:

> The status of the warden – or lack of status – has been inferred as a restraint preventing involvement by secondary teachers in particular. Status can be achieved in a variety of ways – by payment, by position in the educational hierarchy or by a sound acquaintance with the relevant field of knowledge. In the case of teachers' centre wardens, this field of knowledge relates perhaps particularly to curriculum studies. It may well have helped if wardens had received special training, for example, by taking an Advanced Diploma in Education. However, if the post were spare time, involving only a small honorarium in remuneration, training could hardly be considered. (p. 16)

We detected some evidence of conflict between advisory staff and full-time teachers' centre leaders. It made us ask what was the distinctive role of the adviser in curriculum development. Is he to initiate and supervise curriculum change in close, perhaps influential, contact with the decision-makers in schools, or is he to respond to initiatives by organizing a support superstructure in which teachers' centres in the area, and teachers, can play a part? Some comments hint at the dilemma:

> Is training and support to be centrally controlled by LEA officers and funds? Or what is the function of teachers' centre leaders, their centres and their finances in this process? (report from adviser, 1971)
>
> I think the strength of the inspectorate (just numerically) determines to some extent the amount of training a local authority can undertake. (inspector interviewed by JR, for evaluation team, 1970)
>
> Although an increased advisory service will help to spread the load of training, whatever form it takes locally, one has to ask about the function of teachers' centres, whether in initiating this work or else continuing it after the advisers have made the first moves. (report from adviser, 1971)

The imaginative enterprise of centres is largely determined by their budget and by the expertise of their leaders. A leader in a multi-purpose centre could not be expected to be competent across the disciplines. Is he then to support developments in areas to which he is personally committed, shaping the programme of the centre in his own image, or is he to step back and take a general management/caretaker role? One solution would be for centre leaders to acquire a new set of skills in curriculum innovation and implementation. We became aware of the dilemma early in the dissemination of the Project:

> The warden may see himself as a facilitator or manager who provides information and arranges an appropriate schedule of meetings, or he may shape a role of deep involvement in a few curriculum areas. (The mobility of centre leaders is a force to reckon with if the warden plays the leading in-service role in any project.) The problem for the curriculum project is the provision of information and experience to equip centre leaders and other local authority personnel to play the various roles they choose in relation to projects. (p. 109)[19]

The following comments illustrate a range of positions held by teachers' centre leaders on this issue:

> The teachers' centre leader is much more of an enabler. He does not see it as his duty to become deeply involved in any particular project. (report by JR, Project team, 1970)

The teachers' centre leader came to the training course and although not directly involved in the local training, comes to meetings whenever he can. He felt it vital that he came to the central course in order to know what the thing is about. He now organizes meetings, sees that the right kind of materials and support are in the background, and ensures that there is adequate communication among schools. (report by J R, Project team, 1970)

I think I'll probably have to be a group leader. Obviously I won't be able to tell until I see who comes along to the meetings whether or not I can foist this off on to them but I do prefer having teachers as group leaders as this enables me to have far more groups going on in the centre at the same time. (centre leader, interviewed by J R, Project team, 1971)

Like most teachers' centres, I think we have too many fingers in too many pies. The result is that activities of this kind suffer from lack of really well thought out preparations because there just is not enough time to give them the thought they deserve. (letter from centre leader, 1970)

Personally I feel it is important to be involved in experiments of this nature rather than to sit on the side-lines, so at the initial meeting of the schools interested I offered to help any school having particular starting problems with regard to staffing. (centre leader, interviewed by J R, Project team, 1971)

I don't want the centre to become too associated with one project to the exclusion of all others, and I want therefore to be careful not to publicize the Project [HCP] in such a way that it might be taken that I am trying to persuade all schools in my area to use it. (centre leader, interviewed by J R, Project team, 1971)

Perhaps the most significant – but little noted – potential of the teachers' centre is its capacity to provide a reference point outside the schools. Teachers struggling with an innovation that runs counter to the prevailing ethos of their school need the leverage of an alternative reference group. A project's central team can serve in this way but teachers' personal contact with the members of a central team is usually occasional and fleeting. To what extent can teachers' centres provide this leverage? In how many areas do both schools and teachers' centres reflect largely the same set of educational values, and what strategies for change would need to be employed in such areas? One must ask whether the appointment of the centre leader should take into account the need for this alternative framework.

In 1967, when LEAs were being encouraged to establish teachers' centres, the Schools Council [20] projected a threefold function:

> . . . the most important is undoubtedly to focus local interest and to give teachers a setting within which new objectives can be discussed and defined, and new ideas, on content and methods in a variety of subjects, can be aired. (para. 16)
>
> A second function of some centres will be complementary to the first: the schools in the area of a local group may be among those which have been formally invited to give new materials their trial before publication. . . . In this respect [their] role will be to give nationally initiated work a solid foundation in widespread teacher experience and judgement. (para. 17)
>
> Thirdly, where teachers locally are not directly involved in the trial of work which is being nationally developed by an institution in their area they should nevertheless be kept informed about research and development in progress elsewhere. If teachers are to participate fully in the work of curriculum review, they need to be made quickly and expertly familiar with important projects as they develop. (para. 18)

We have seen the centres take on an additional task – the task of organizing and providing accommodation and resources for local induction courses – and we have been sensitive to the difficulties encountered as centre leaders were drawn, tentatively or confidently, into the dissemination practices of a national curriculum development project.

Colleges, institutes and departments of education

STRATEGY FOR INVOLVEMENT

Attention to colleges, institutes and departments was not part of the Schools Council's brief to the Humanities Project team but it seemed important that the Project should be made accessible to them.

Four pilot colleges did the reconnaissance work and presented reports of their experience at a small conference (36 participants and the Project team) in July 1969 (reported by Evans).[21] The aim of the conference was:

> . . . for the team to present the work of the Project, making explicit some of its difficulties and implications; to provide an opportunity for tutors engaged in initial and in-service training of teachers to help the Project team by considering whether there were any ways in which colleges and institutes would want to be associated with the work of the Project. (p. 57)

Six questions were put to the conference in the final sessions. They now seem a strange blend of general policy issues and specific research problems:

1. If the work was transmitting teaching through experience, were there any implications for teacher education?
2. Should packs of materials be available to colleges and institutes?
3. Could colleges and institutes help with research on two questions: when to introduce evidence to a discussion and what is the effect of introducing evidence to a discussion?
4. What questions should the Project be trying to answer from the schools?
5. What is the place of the 'chairman' style of teaching technique in a college? Given that style of work, is there a different response, say, for music and literature?
6. In-service training? (p. 61)

At this conference a working party with four college, two institute and two Project representatives was elected. The 'urgent first task was to devise a regular means of communication between colleges, institutes and the Project'. One concrete result of the deliberations of the working party was a larger conference (55 participants and the Project team) in July 1970 (reported by Fowler).[22] The working party's circular letter described the proposed training course in this way:

> For people genuinely interested in the application of the approach of the Project and the implications for training institutions, both in the professional training of students and teachers and in the training of students themselves at their own level. The members of such a course would act as trainers within their own institutions. (October 1969)

The conference chairman and *rapporteur*, Vice-Principal of his college, took a firm line:

> The time was overdue for colleges, departments and institutes to assume responsibility for looking at the experiment and its implications . . . it was important for colleges to respond to change in the schools. (p. 68)[22]

But it was difficult for the conference to make firm policy recommendations; one problem was the status of participants within their own institutions – they faced much the same problem as teachers who come to a central training course, alone and unsupported, and go back to persuade or convince their head that something should be done about the Project:

> It was suggested that there should be appropriate machinery for reporting conferences back to academic boards even if delegates were not academic board members. (p. 70)

There were three action proposals:

a that there should be an exchange of information: colleges need to know about LEA activities; LEAs needed to know of college interest.

Copies of LEA dissemination plans were subsequently sent to interested colleges and at the same time LEAs were told 'which colleges were represented at the courses in case there might be some mutual advantage in arranging a dialogue'. (letter to LEAs, JR, Project team, August 1970);

b that the Project team at their new centre in East Anglia would act as 'clearing house for correspondence, enquiries about speakers, etc'.

There has in fact been little call on our time for this service.

c that the initiative for a further conference should be in the hands of the colleges.

No such conference was arranged. Instead, lecturers apply for places at the central training courses where they work alongside teachers and LEA personnel.

ROLES AND RESPONSES

The response of colleges to the Project suggests that colleges have two roles in externally developed curriculum innovation: the role of user, even as schools are users, and the role of local disseminator, even as LEAs are local disseminators. We identified four patterns of response: the first two showing the colleges primarily as users, that is, introducing the Project as part of the curriculum with the aim of increasing students' understanding of the issues explored; the last two showing the colleges more as disseminators, that is, treating the Project as an example of curriculum innovation or setting up and taking part in courses to train people to work with the Project in schools.

a (i) Colleges introduce the Project whole, attempting to work with materials and methods as part of a social studies or general education course, with issues discussed at student level and with the implications for the Project in schools as a secondary consideration;

(ii) colleges use the *Education* materials in a Humanities Project discussion setting, as an introduction to issues in education.

b Colleges store the materials in the library or resource centre, and students and staff draw on the materials to support their teaching, in particular subject areas or in thematic project work.

c Colleges encourage students to examine the Project, perhaps in a curriculum studies course:

(i) theoretically, looking at the Project as an example of innovation – looking at the educational principles which inform it, at other projects in the humanities area, at the aims/objectives issue, at the approach to evaluation, at the institutional resistances to innovation;

(ii) practically, that is with the aim of preparing students to work on the Project in the schools. Students may or may not observe the Project in operation in schools in the ATO; they may or may not attempt the work themselves on teaching practice.

d Colleges organize in-service courses and these can reflect the emphasis outlined in **c**(i) and **c**(ii) above; or colleges contribute to the dissemination programmes organized by local authorities. They usually act as 'trainers' but it is not inconceivable to find students and staff involved in an attempt to mount a specialist evaluation study.

The college as user

The problems are similar in some respects to those that confront the school as user. There is the problem of training staff. To judge from the number of college representatives at central training courses (relatively small or surprisingly large, depending on whether or not one sees the colleges as having any obligation to involve themselves in curriculum development), it seems that college lecturers who plan to introduce the Project are more likely to rely on the self-training programme than on the central courses for their understanding of the experiment.

Resistances to the Project and difficulties in its implementation are likely to be as intense in colleges as they are in schools. A student comments on the introduction of HCP in his college:

> The failure [of HCP in the college] reflects the type of institution into which the course has been introduced. In an atmosphere essentially authoritarian and paternalistic there is suddenly presented a surface move to democracy. Lecturers participate on a first-name basis, an attenuation of their authority which many do not normally allow. The student is released from the paternalism pervading the whole atmosphere of college and told to discuss on an equal, men and women, basis.
>
> This happens in a situation where there are accepted rules such as no (or muted) contradiction of lecturers, behaviour, times to be in at lodgings. Acquiescence, not stimulating enquiry, is the general order of things. . . .
>
> The failure of humanities – at the student level – to promote rational discussion and thinking, its primary objective, may be seen as a failure on the part of the college and the students – the students, most of whom have just left the authoritarian situation of the school, for acquiescing to the general apathy and intellectual standard, and the college for perpetuating a less restricted, but comparable, school situation. Stenhouse comments on the attitude of teachers: 'If we are to move from this attitude of custodial containment to the desire to help pupils cope with life after they have left school, we must at some time wean them from dependence on our authority.' How much, one wonders, does this also refer to the college of education? (*Times Educational Supplement*, 27 August 1971)

One might construe this attack as evidence of the need to introduce the Project in colleges as a course in its own right. But there is an overriding set of problems. These arise out of the structure of courses in colleges of education. There are generally four kinds of activity in a college curriculum: main and subsidiary subject courses; curriculum courses (brief introductions to subjects other than those studied academically in main and subsidiary courses); education; teaching practice. In many colleges, the education course has been structured on the basis of a claim that the study of education is reducible to the constituent disciplines: sociology, psychology and philosophy (and sometimes history). There may also be an element of comparative studies in education.

The problem (and this is one that faces schools too) is, 'Where would the Project fit?' In the constituent disciplines approach, there is no obvious place for a study of new curricula; nor are there more than a few humanities or general studies content and methods courses. Often then there is no obvious organizational structure to enable colleges to look at new curricula. Nevertheless, some colleges have chosen to examine and work on the Humanities Project with their students. The Project may slip in under the wings of the religious education or English department, educationists may get a philosophic grip on it, or it may figure in some of the new curriculum studies courses where two or three projects are looked at in some depth.

The involvement of colleges in nationally developed projects is controversial. Some would argue that it is the responsibility of the LEA to introduce teachers to innovations that have been adopted locally. There are to date over one hundred and forty projects funded by the Schools Council and the Nuffield Foundation. Colleges would have difficulty in establishing criteria by which they would select particular projects to present to students. A college might concentrate, in initial courses, on what generalizes from project to project – such as discovery and enquiry approaches to learning – or it might instead focus on one or two projects which exemplify significant styles and problems in curriculum development. Such courses would be orientation courses rather than training courses; they would not equip a student to teach a particular project in school but they would heighten his awareness of what was at stake in different teaching approaches.

The college as local disseminator

Colleges have contributed most to the dissemination of the Project through in-service training. In some areas, college staff work alongside LEA personnel and teachers on local induction courses. There has been some evidence of prejudice towards college lecturers, which seems to be based on the image of the college teacher as 'an expert without a classroom':

> He took a dominant and sometimes intrusive part in the discussion compared with other members of the training panel who assumed a retiring role to allow the teachers to air their problems. (report of a local training course by HS, evaluation team, 1971)

Another problem is that there is often no easy passage for college lecturers to and from the teachers' centres. In some areas, the centre is a no-man's-land as far as the colleges are concerned. The growth of professional centres, which may be located in college premises, may ease this particular problem.

As an alternative to participating in local dissemination activities, college and institute staff have set up meetings that supplement local courses, offering regionally what, for financial and administrative reasons, it would be difficult to offer locally – a panel of speakers from different parts of the country, discussion with members of a project team working in the Humanities area, videotape recording and play-back facilities. Yet another pattern of involvement has developed: in areas where there is no organized communication, training or support activity at local level, the colleges or institutes have assumed an almost exclusive responsibility for HCP in-service courses.

Her Majesty's Inspectorate

It is probably rather casual to think of Her Majesty's Inspectorate as an alternative dissemination agency. As far as we know, there has been no policy decision about its role in relation to national development projects. During the lifetime of the Humanities Project there were, however, two formal links with the Inspectorate. Their representative served on the Project's consultative committee, and, secondly, the director of the Project was invited to speak to a meeting of HMIs in London in 1968.

There is insufficient evidence to support useful general speculation about the possible roles and effects of the Inspectorate in the dissemination of nationally developed curriculum work. The Humanities Project is controversial and is likely, as the Project handbook[7] points out, to 'divide pupils, parents and teachers'. It is in fact likely to divide any group, including Inspectors and Schools Council field officers, that does not have a policy that sets official response above the personal response of the individual.

Any HMI choosing to involve himself in the Project would need – as would any other individual – to acquire sufficient understanding of it to make his interest profitable to the system.

Schools Council field officers

An informal link with the Inspectorate was through the field officer team which, during the lifetime of the Project, was led by an HMI. For a time there was a regular exchange of information between the field officers and the Project team. But the officers are on short-term appointment; their exits and their entrances are phased, and latterly the Project failed to seek meetings with the changed field officer team and new field officers did not seek places, as some of their predecessors had done, on Project training courses. By 1972 the Humanities Project may have become 'old hat' and the officers' attention was probably with the Council's current projects.

Our feeling was that field officers, as a group, could make a more positive contribution to the dissemination of Schools Council work and to the Council's understanding of the problems of dissemination in different areas of the country. Their strengths include a knowledge of the local scene. Some officers have, as individuals, found a way of harnessing this strength in dissemination, helping to build, locally and regionally, support networks and regional associations. They know the people and the places; they have access and some authority. Now, at the level of helping to maintain and repair these local and regional networks for innovating teachers, their efforts would be invaluable but, given the number of projects in schools, it would be invidious for them to select particular projects for particular attention; energetic support for the Humanities Project dissemination programme would certainly lie outside their remit.

Our relationship with the field officers highlighted two problems; that of maintaining contact with a group of people whose membership is not stable; and that of ensuring that people in official positions who could, individually or as a group, contribute to the dissemination of curriculum ideas are sufficiently well informed for their contribution to be constructive.

The publisher

Heinemann Educational Books has offices in Melbourne and Auckland. In 1972 Paul Richardson (the director responsible for the Humanities material) spent six months in these two places on an exchange visit.

He took with him articles about the Project, some materials, and a videotape of work in the classroom. He had kept closely in touch with the Project since first publication in May 1970 and was reasonably well informed about the problems and potential of its introduction in schools. He talked about the Project at both formal and informal meetings. There was, by a publisher's yardstick, an encouraging response. Small quantities of materials had already been sold to Australia and New Zealand. Now the possibility was raised of a more extensive and systematic introduction of the Project. The publisher was, in effect, acting as disseminator in these two countries. Why not in the UK?

We had made no place in our dissemination programme for the publisher and the publishing house's sales representatives. Perhaps we suffered from exaggerated sensibilities about promotion; in our own communication about the Project we took an explicitly anti-promotion line. Our aim was to give people an opportunity to make informed decisions about the experiment. Open days and training courses were attempts to marshal evidence and at the same time to ensure that participants became more discerning in their judgement. On such occasions, our line was this: 'If at the end of the course you go away secure in a better understanding of the Project but with the realization that it is not an appropriate experiment for you as an individual or for your school as an institution, then this course will have been effective.' Despite our intentions, this line may in fact have been a soft sell. Interested but tentative customers were so beguiled by our honesty in exposing the difficulties of the work that they were persuaded to commit themselves to the Project. We were intent on fostering independent, grounded judgement, but we were unconsciously playing the promotion game, where it seems that honesty is the best policy.

The main dilemma for the publisher grew out of the assumption that teachers needed to be trained to undertake the Project (an assumption which the results of the evaluation team's measurement programme showed to be a sound one). A publicity campaign that led to rapid and widespread purchase could have been disadvantageous to the Project and to the publisher: the frustration of teachers who became involved in the Project without understanding it, and without support, could produce an anti-sales backlash. It would take time for notions of training to penetrate the consciousness of the system and it would take still longer to set up the machinery for adequate local training and 'after-care'. Heinemann's promotional work has been well-judged: comprehensive and regular circulation of information, varied in its presentation (for each major mailing the handouts were re-designed) and elegant rather than blatant. Sales are being maintained even though the Project ended officially three years ago.

How did Heinemann set about publicizing the Project? Throughout the programme, there was close and helpful co-operation with the Project team. Heinemann passed on to us any information that might contribute to our understanding of the national pattern of demand. Paul Richardson attended many of the Project's consultative committee meetings, and his colleague came to some open days, and to sessions at some training courses.

Heinemann was responsible, of course, for the first public and private communication about the Project. In 1969 they circularized all appropriate educational institutions – a circulation of about eight thousand. The Project, through the Schools Council, had only written to Chief Education Officers at that stage. Then, in May 1970, it called a press conference to mark the publication of the first two collections of materials. This is the image of the Project first presented to the public through the national press:

> The most ambitious and expensive of all the projects backed by the Schools Council was officially launched on Monday. The Humanities Project, and its publishers, Heinemann, put on the market boxes of materials, weighing half a hundredweight and costing £30 each. (*Times Educational Supplement*)

> Lawrence Stenhouse's outfit – the Schools Council/Nuffield Humanities Project team – is to get a new lease of life when its three-year term runs out at the end of the year. Then it switches its base from south London to the University of East Anglia, where it will take on the august title: The Centre for Applied Research in Curriculum and Teaching. The extension of the team's work sets the seal of approval on the Project which was set up in 1967 to seek out ways of handling difficult topics. (*Education*)

> Mr Lawrence Stenhouse, the project director, said he thought it would provide a 'vehicle for a new kind of relationship with pupils'. Already, more than one thousand schools have expressed interest in the project. (*Guardian*)

> But much more controversial than the content is the technique that the team suggests, for that demands a radical and complex change of

position for the traditionally subject-centred and didactic secondary-school teacher. . . .

It won't be easy, if teachers don't grasp that the method increases their responsibility. . . .

And there are obviously logistical problems with the mounds of polythene packs produced by the project. ('The best decision of the last school year was to store the stuff in a boys' lavatory', one teacher said.)* One suspects on the evidence of that school that a lot of teachers either don't or won't understand what is being demanded of them. . . .

It's not for nothing that this project has the biggest funds of any Schools Council effort. But if the project's essentially civilized aim is to be realized the whole of a school needs to be alerted to its implications. (*New Society*)

Having once been caught in the crossfire of an argument between Mr Stenhouse and one of his critics, I have no intention of taking sides on the question of whether the Humanities Project approach amounts to a valid teaching approach or not. What is certain, though, is that it makes a radical re-valuation of the teacher's role, and for that reason the introduction to the Project, contained in each pack, deserves to be studied. No doubt teachers' centres will be receiving copies of this, and I recommend it as essential reading for all teachers who still have more than five years to serve. It may well prove to be a blueprint for the nature of their work in the future, at whatever level they teach. (*Teachers World*)

To Lawrence Stenhouse and his team, these materials are largely irrelevant: 'any publisher can produce materials'. Nor are they specially concerned with humanities, or with young school leavers. For the last few years, working in the jungle where all curriculum projects work – producing materials, training teachers to use them, selling them to local authorities and schools, evaluating their effects in the classroom – they have been stalking extremely large and powerful and threatening ideas about what education ought to be, what it is in practice, and how you set about changing schools and the curriculum to close the gap between the two. . . .

* The reporter had previously visited one HCP experimental school.

It all sounds very straightforward until you start trying to put it into schools. . . .

The project got a lot of criticism over the idea of neutrality. . . .

It would be a bad mistake to judge the value of the Humanities Project on their prototype materials, and not on the force of their ideas. (*Times Educational Supplement* leader)

And headlines read:

PROJECT COSTS £230 000
CHARGING INTO CONTROVERSIAL AREAS
HUMANITY UNWELCOME
TEACHER CAN PLUG IN

How did the Project come to work with Heinemann Educational? The Schools Council customarily holds round-the-table meetings where 'mid-wife' publishers can examine the 'pregnant' project. Interested publishers receive more detailed information about the planned materials and may then submit publishing proposals for examination by the Council in consultation with the project team. Heinemann was found to be the most suitable of the publishers who drew up proposals for the Humanities Curriculum Project (and they also had an established list of books on education that offered an outlet for the research studies that the Project team were planning). Arrangements were therefore made for Heinemann to publish the Project's materials.

This may have been seen as a risky undertaking. There had already been some public debate about the Project, and the materials themselves presented technical problems and design constraints: the materials were loose-leaf; the team did not want typographical or design 'embroidery' that would destroy the relationship between the 'evidence' and the source materials from which it was taken; colour was to be used only as an index of form (journalism, drama, poetry, for example); the materials were likely to go straight into a school's resource system (albeit the drawers of a filing cabinet) and elaborate packaging would therefore be an expensive waste. On the other hand, the Project was from the Schools Council stud – it was well sired – and it had been generated as part of the raising of the school leaving age programme; there were likely to be backers. As time passed the sense of risk that had earlier been experienced seemed to fade:

It was, therefore, certainly the case that a number of commercial publishers were highly sceptical about the viability of the project in commercial terms, and it was no doubt regarded by many people as something of a gamble. This was not of course our view, although we ourselves did not expect sales of the order of those which have actually been achieved. (letter from the publisher, March 1973)

What features of Heinemann's style of operation affected the dissemination of the Project? There were two. First, Heinemann decided not to produce sample packs of materials. This decision, although probably made on economic grounds, did in fact serve the image of the Project: a practice of answering enquiries with generous bundles of materials would be likely to reinforce the already widespread assumption that projects are about materials rather than methods. The cheapest project purchase – and the best introduction to the experiment – was the Project handbook at 35p. The next cheapest purchase was a teacher's (or reference) set of materials; these cost about £14 per theme. At this price, people had to think before making an investment. Second, Heinemann did not work through retailers; it sold direct to consumers and it had a team of representatives, each serving regions of England and Wales, with one representative serving Scotland.

One thing that the Project team underestimated in dissemination was the commitment of Heinemann's representatives and the pressures they were subjected to. We should have recognized earlier the weakness and strength of their potential contribution to the dissemination of the Project; representatives should have been better briefed and better supported by the Project team. Our inattention can only be explained in terms of our preoccupation with LEAs and schools.

Representatives would talk about the Project with teachers in schools. They were also, from time to time, invited to set up an exhibition of Project materials for local introductory or training courses. In both settings, representatives were likely to be asked questions which they could not easily answer, and since many people had no opportunity to air their suspicions or grievances to a member of the Project team, the representatives were seen as a surrogate team and were by turns interrogated, praised and cursed. Or so they said at a meeting in September 1972. They had talked about their 'complaining customers', who felt let down by the difficulty of their materials.

> Some were disturbed by teachers' readiness to dismiss the 'Newsom group'. There were some wry confessions: 'If teachers think that two-thirds of the materials are beyond the grasp of fourth-year pupils, I say, "Give two-thirds of the materials to your sixth forms, use one

third with the early leavers and you've two projects for the price of one".' The wryness indicated an understanding of the tension between the urge to sell and the recognition that purchase is not always appropriate. Some representatives told me roundly that HCP was different, the materials didn't carry the message and that the handbook was the best introduction. Their degree of commitment to understanding was greater than I felt would be possible. They clearly wanted to take responsibility for a stronger dissemination role, and a request for a training course came from them. (report of the meeting by JR, Project team)

As a result of the meeting, we invited representatives to Project open days, and prepared information sheets for them. A list of common questions was then drawn up by the representatives and we were faced with the problem of helping them to cope with the questions without recourse to over-rehearsed and over-simplified answers. The questions they needed help with were often basic and deceptively simple:

What is the Project all about?

How does the teacher use this material?

How does the teacher fit into the scheme of things – as a teacher and as chairman?

Could the extrovert, vocal pupil dominate the discussion to the detriment of the shyer pupil if the teacher remains impartial and does not take part?

What department should use the Project?

Which groups of students should be involved – school leavers, sixth form?

Can the teacher miss out the more difficult bits in the materials or will this ruin the topic being studied?

Can the packs be used without the films and tapes?

Can individual issues be rearranged within topics or is there a definite order to follow?

Are any topics more suitable for boys/girls/mixed classes?

Is there a proper order for the topics?

Is there likely to be a syllabus written for HCP? How do teachers evaluate their sessions?

> Is any supplementary or additional material going to be produced or is this all?
>
> How much teaching time should be devoted to the Project? Does each topic have a definite time limit?'

Our answers to these and other questions are reproduced in Appendix E.

The evaluation programme

Evaluation is traditionally an instrument of dissemination. It may measure the extent to which a project achieves its objectives and so provide reassurance to the consumer. In the Humanities Project the pattern is broken and the functional relationship between Project and evaluation is re-invented. Overall, the potential contribution to dissemination is much greater. The objectives model, with its range of intended learning outcomes, was not appropriate for the Humanities Project. Evaluation had to re-orient itself:

> The major point of evaluation was to make the Project useable and to enable people to make informed judgements about it; to expose its flexibility, its adaptability; to communicate notions about the conditions under which it is likely to prosper or to fail.*

The evaluation team in addition to its background studies of response in LEAs undertook case-studies of the Project in experimental and dissemination schools; these studies show the impact of the Project in particular circumstances. The case-studies are complemented by a measurement programme. Neither element is intended to stand alone; each cautions the interpretation of the other. The target for the data is decision-makers: heads and teachers, LEA officers, parents and students, examining boards and employers, the Project's sponsors, the Project team itself.

Evaluation affected both the nature of the Project and the style of its presentation. The evaluation studies conducted during the experimental period, 1968–70, underlined the crucial importance to innovation of support, both within the school and within the LEA. Support meant the

* Quotations in this section are from statements by Barry MacDonald, director of the evaluation team, in an interview with JR, Project team, May 1973. For a brief account of the evaluation programme, see Barry MacDonald's contribution to *Evaluation in Curriculum Development: Twelve Case Studies*, Schools Council Research Studies (Macmillan Education, 1973), pp. 80–90.

kind of understanding that leads to appropriate planning and realistic expectations. Further, the evaluation programme stimulated a critical, reflective attitude, among the Project team, towards the logic of the Project's design. It was the evaluation team that asked experimental teachers to record classroom discussion; it was from these recordings that hypotheses for the self-training programme were derived. In ways such as these the evaluation activities were formative of what was to be disseminated in 1970. And the evaluation team helped to establish the tone of public communication:

> We knew enough from the [experimental] schools to know that the initial experience of the Project is extremely tough and dismaying. It was clearly true that unless people went in with realistic expectations, the thing would have no chance of surviving. . . . I have absolutely no doubt that the adoption of any perspective on this project other than a realistic one would have been quite disastrous.

In a sense, the evaluation team was the Project's super-ego; in our public appearances, Big Brother MacDonald was watching us. The Project team respected the perspective and values of the evaluation unit: a common purpose was to put forward a fair picture of what had happened.

> The evaluation [team] was more able, more likely and more free to concentrate on difficulties and problems [in the implementation of the Project] – the failures and the conditions of failure – than the Project team which is vulnerable to criticism and to pressures. . . . One function of the evaluation was to serve as a form of legitimation of claims made by the Project people in dissemination, and so to raise the credibility of the Project and to provide a check for people wishing to question what was being said to them in dissemination. . . . The role that we had to perform in relation to dissemination was to check and check again what was being communicated, whether it was accurate or not.

In style and tone the Project team and evaluation team drew towards each other as the dissemination period continued. The lack of distinction was apparent in some of the service functions: the evaluation team made videotapes of classroom work which were borrowed for central and local training courses; they produced a bulletin (the HCP *Evaluation Report*) and a series of articles that contributed to the creation of a community of persons in contact with one another. And through the case-study of schools, they gave to innovating teachers – although on a very small scale – the support of interested observation.

> Had there been no evaluation, the dissemination would still have been the same. It would have been slightly less competent on the grounds that any additional person to any group of people is likely to increase the competence, making a general contribution to the intellectual pool. . . . Things were done by us and if they hadn't been done by us it would have been necessary for you to do them.

Although the evaluation unit published fairly extensively during the life of the project, the major audience aimed at in these publications was the people in the schools and LEAs already involved, or those in the shallows of involvement. Therefore, in terms of informing decision-makers at large it is possible to argue that the evaluation was of limited effectiveness. It was not until well after the end of the Project that its main reports began to appear,[14, 23] and in 1975 some are still in preparation. These are reports which might influence the policy-makers in addition to the decision-makers.

The experimental designs of projects are partly to blame for such time-lags. The pilot and public phases are end-on; there is no breathing space for the evaluation team to collect and present its thoughts in readiness for the last round of dissemination decisions. The process is still more complicated when the evaluation teams feels, as it did on the HCP, that it has inherited a design based on the assumption that its main studies must be conducted in dissemination schools: the experimental schools are atypical in terms of selection and support, contact and communication. The evaluation team, caught in the time-trap, found that its aim was unrealistic. It managed an adjustment which would accommodate the late publication of its main reports:

> We shifted our attention to try to produce information that would feed repeating decisions. . . . We tended to look at the Project as being illustrative of new curricula, and the kind of values they would create, so that our information would be relevant to future decisions rather than to this particular one.

It will be interesting to observe the impact of the main evaluation report when it is finally ready to be published – with luck, in the sixth year of dissemination and over three years after the Project officially ended. Maybe it will make its biggest contribution to dissemination by providing a booster when the momentum of the dissemination wave is beginning to decline.

Journals and the Press

The Project has been the subject of very many articles and papers. It has provoked written response from a wide range of people, both in this country and, to some extent, abroad. It is interesting to speculate on the effect of this attention, in print, on the dissemination of the Project. It was helpful to the extent that it focused on controversy and thereby served to clarify issues and to delineate the dimensions of the Project. The debate in the Press was often a public projection of the clash of values that the Project was provoking more quietly up and down the country. News coverage sensitized the team to the popular and potent lines of attack – and served to keep the Project in the public eye.

Throughout the experimental period, 1968–70, publicity was kept to a minimum. The Project team was anxious to protect its 150 teachers from external scrutiny during the difficult formative stages of the work, and we were concerned not to create demands for materials that could not be met. Reference in the press was mainly to statements made by the Project team at educational conferences. Some lively correspondence usually resulted. What is interesting, throughout the period of the Project, is the range of participants in the debate. The Project had become a talking point. The height of its journalistic notoriety came in 1972, when the Schools Council decided that it could not approve publication of the pack of materials on race relations and advocated further development work in the field. 'Council blackout' was one of the headlines.

Public examinations

During the experimental phase of the Project, almost half the schools involved had either devised CSE syllabuses or were planning syllabuses for later use. The raising of the school leaving age to 16 in 1972 meant that all pupils would be in school during the year of the GCE O-level and CSE examinations. With the rise in the number of pupils eligible and available for examinations, it was expected that there would be an increase in the number of pupils undertaking public examinations. There was no reason to suppose that the Humanities Project would be exempt from the effects of this trend.

For many schools, the public examination is a means of giving status and respectability to a curriculum innovation in the eyes of pupils, teachers not involved in the innovative work, and parents and employers. Curriculum innovation that is not located within a traditional subject area may not be easily accommodated by the existing machinery for examinations. We were aware that teachers interested in submitting Humanities Project work for public examination were likely to need help.

We were also concerned about the problem of internal assessment: teachers would want to reassure themselves that the strategies they were exploring were furthering the aim of the Project, that is, to help students develop an understanding of social situations and human acts and of the controversial value issues that they raise. It is not uncommon for teachers to express aims in terms of understanding. In English and in history teaching, for instance, 'understanding' appears to be accepted as an appropriate aim and there is little evidence of distress at the problem of interpreting understanding. It was the novelty of the Humanities Project that prompted considerable reflection, among the Project team and among teachers attending training courses, on the nature of understanding* and on the problems of assessment.

In 1970, the Project team nominated one of its members to take special responsibility for assessment, and it approved the setting up, in the same year, of a working party on Examining in the Humanities. This working party met three times: in April 1970, June 1970 and January 1971. Its membership was drawn from the Project team (four), the examining boards (four),† from the Project experimental schools (three), and from the Schools Council (five). The working party sanctioned the preparation of a book which would give teachers some practical help and raise issues in the assessment of Project work.‡ The working party's discussions served to delineate many of these issues and to identify areas where guidance might be needed. It was crucial to the dissemination of the Project that boards should be sensitive to the problems of assessment in the humanities and that teachers should realize where they might have to take initiatives.

* John Elliott, *The Nature of Understanding*, Centre for Applied Research in Education, University of East Anglia, 1971 (unpublished paper).

† Metropolitan Regional Examinations Board, Associated Lancashire Schools Examining Board, Southern Regional Examinations Board, North Western Secondary School Examinations Board.

‡ Not yet published, but a pamphlet on assessment, with examples of CSE syllabuses, *CSE (Mode III) and the Humanities Curriculum Project*, is available from CARE, University of East Anglia.

A paper prepared for the working party identified the following areas of concern.

Devising the syllabus (for CSE examinations, Modes II and III)
It was necessary to specify aim, content, and criteria for assessment. The paper underlined the danger, in enquiry work, of specifying too precisely in advance what the coverage was to be. It proposed instead that boards accept *examples* of the kind of issues that might be explored and of the kind of outcomes that might emerge. The paper also discussed the balance of methods of assessment – work continuously assessed, course-work in the form of a project or folio, an end-of-course examination. It took a position on the assessment of discussion. Some teachers argue that if more time is spent on discussion than other activities, then it ought to carry at least some proportion of the marks. In a note prepared by the Project team for a meeting of the working party, teachers were advised against such a move:

> In this connection we feel it is important that discussion, the core activity of the work, should not be assessed in the public sense. There are a number of reasons for our view. First it is undesirable that students should feel encouraged to 'perform'. Discussion work if it is to be successful depends upon a certain integrity of discourse, a concern to establish the nature of things rather than to create an impression. This implies that students feel free to experiment and make mistakes; for this reason many teachers have remarked that reflectiveness rather than argumentativeness is the ideal climate of discussion. Secondly, one of the assumptions on which discussion is based is that diversity of view rather than consensus is desirable. If students are aware that the neutral chairman is making judgements they may feel that certain points of view, certain modes of expression may be more acceptable to him than others. However mistaken this point of view, it may be difficult for some students, particularly those prone to conformism, to resist it. Finally, some students may decide that in an atmosphere of evaluation the best policy is to remain silent. Given these possibilities, all of which would be unfavourable to discussion, we conclude that discussion should be exempt from public evaluation and known to be exempt. For similar reasons we would resist the suggestion that the teacher should include a subjective impression of students' progress as part of the overall evaluation. It

seems to us important that the criteria of assessment are made as explicit as possible and relate to performance demonstrated in a range of definite outcomes. Private judgements divorced from outcomes may add to students' mystification and increase their uncertainty as to the nature of desirable standards. (J H, Project team, June 1970)

Moderation and certification

The working party recognized that the existing social science syllabuses, to which Humanities Project syllabuses seemed likely to be assimilated, were not entirely appropriate for Project work. Special panels might need to be set up and it might be important for the experienced Project teachers from the experimental schools to take on responsibilities for moderation until familiarity with the Project was more widely established.

It was anticipated that there would be problems of certification. Schools that were spending considerably more time on the Project than others were likely to seek multiple certification. The Project's handbook[7] refers to humanities courses which cross the subject boundaries between English, history, geography, religious studies and social studies. If, under multiple certification, Project syllabuses were submitted to each panel in turn, the scrutiny might be conducted in too subject-oriented a manner:

> It is not suggested that such perspectives are the wrong ones to encourage; indeed specialists may quite legitimately insist that they are not lost sight of. What is suggested however is that few humanities syllabuses would survive scrutiny of this sort. (internal paper by Project team)

The Project team was, then, concerned to help examining boards and teachers understand what was at stake in public examination of the work. We were particularly responsive to a move by a GCE board towards acceptance of an HCP syllabus. The implications of this move might be considerable: it could mean that students normally segregated into GCE and CSE streams could work together as a mixed-ability group on a course leading, for all students, to public examination.

To examine or not to examine

It is interesting to speculate whether the difficulties of devising appropriate procedures for assessment will result in a gradual adulteration of the distinctive quality of the Project; indeed, whether the pressures of the public examination system are largely responsible in our system for what is commonly perceived as the last phase in the process of innovation – institutionalization, or assimilation through acceptance into routine.

It is important to emphasize the fact that public examination of the Humanities work has been a highly controversial issue. The Project team has tried to support both those schools that are anxious to undertake public examination and those that have introduced the work into that part of the curriculum which is protected from examination pressures. We have tried to help the expedient put their case (by the expedient we mean those who see the examination as a necessary means to gaining status, in their institution, for the Project); and we have tried to help the idealists explain their position (the idealists tend to argue that public examination will inevitably destroy the integrity of the work). At training courses, our task has often been to rescue the expedient from being devoured by the idealist lions.

IX. Postscript

A national training and support programme

In March 1975, two and a half years after the end of the funded life-span of the Project, a national training and support programme was established on the initiative of a former member of the central team. It is managed by people who have considerable experience of the Project, as teachers or as organizers and leaders of training courses. The group has ten members:

Ron Bland, from Bishop Lonsdale College of Education, Derbyshire. He worked as joint editor of one of the packs of materials and has run training courses on HCP at the Loughborough Summer School;

Mike Bray, from Cliftonville School, Northampton. He was a pilot HCP teacher, has six years of classroom experience with the Project, has jointly run training courses at Loughborough and has been on the staff team at a national course.

John Bull, from Ashmead School, Reading. He has five years of classroom experience with the Project and has been on the staff team at national and local courses.

Alan Dale, from Astor School, Dover. He was a pilot teacher and has five years of classroom experience with the Project; he joined the central team for six months to visit schools during the dissemination phase and has been on the staff team at national courses.

Richard Exton, from Tower Hamlets School, London. He was a pilot teacher and has six years of classroom experience of the Project. He has been on the staff team at national and local courses and is currently secretary of the London HCP Association.

Peggy Hooton, who became involved in 1970 when she was a teacher at the Irthing Valley School, Cumberland. She has run courses in different parts of the country and has been on the staff team at national courses. She is now Tutor for In-service Training at the Institute of Education, University of Newcastle.

Tina Reay, who is secretary to the group. She has worked at the Centre for Applied Research in Education at the University of East Anglia on the Ford Teaching Project in Enquiry and Discovery Learning.

Jean Rudduck, from the Centre for Applied Research in Education. She was a member of the Project's central team and has been on the staff of national and local courses.

Harold Taylor from Gloucestershire Local Education Authority. He first attended a national training course in 1971 and has since organized a programme of local training and support.

Sheelah Wilson, from Stockport Local Education Authority. As a former Schools Council field officer she built a close contact with the Project.

The structures which should sustain access to the Project's ideas and experiences have, in some parts of the country, been weakened by such events as local authority reorganization and the consequent shifts of responsibility within the advisory service, or the general mobility of teachers (heightened, sometimes, by problems of secondary-school reorganization). There were also increased opportunities for involvement in other projects in the humanities area and a consequent deflection, in some places, of attention and resources from HCP.

At the same time other events argued a possible upsurge of interest in HCP: the references in the Bullock report[24] to the Project in relation to reading skills; the, on balance, optimistic analysis by Gulliford and Widlake in *Teaching Materials for Disadvantaged Children*[25] of the use of HCP in situations which had not been directly monitored by the team; a more general acceptance of the importance of discussion-based work; and a more general interest in work where thinking and discussion is disciplined by evidence. In 1970 the strongest line of appeal for the Project was probably its contribution to raising of the school leaving age programmes. In 1975 that appeal is less captivating and it seems that these other aspects of the Project could well prove powerful in harnessing current interests. Finally, and most importantly, there is the Project's relevance to the perennial and deeply significant problem of authority and relationships in the classroom, and it is here that HCP offers insights and strategies that will not easily be supplanted.

Such were the reflections of the national training and support group at its first meeting. It set itself the following tasks in an attempt to understand present HCP activity and to anticipate likely needs:

a to maintain a yearly or twice-yearly national training course and to extend the nucleus of teachers capable of taking staff roles at national courses (and therefore, it is hoped, able to organize and staff effective local courses);

b to arrange an occasional 'review of training' conference for people who have training responsibilities at local and regional levels or have the task of inducting colleagues in a school setting where there is no local support programme;

c to gather edited videotapes of Project work in classrooms, and other materials, as resources for local and regional meetings;

d to explore the feasibility of responding to requests for some up-dating of the Project's materials;

e to compile a directory of persons and institutions actively involved in the Project in different areas of the country, and to make this available.

The meetings of the planning group are covered by an allowance from the Nuffield Foundation's share of royalties from the published materials (administered through a trust fund); the programme of activities is supported from a small grant made by the Schools Council.

References

1. M. HERRON, 'On teacher perception and curricular innovation', *Curriculum Theory Network*, monograph supplement, 1971. (Ontario Institute for Studies in Education.)
2. *Choosing a Curriculum for the Young School Leaver* (Schools Council Working Paper 33). Evans/Methuen Educational, 1971.
3. *Society and the Young School Leaver: a humanities programme in preparation for the raising of the school leaving age* (Schools Council Working Paper No. 11). HMSO, 1967.
4. *Half our Future*: a report of the Central Advisory Council for Education (England) [The Newsom Report]. HMSO, 1963.
5. *Raising the School Leaving Age: a co-operative programme of research and development* (Schools Council Working Paper No. 2). HMSO, 1965.
6. D. WARWICK (ed.) *Integrated Studies in the Secondary School.* University of London Press, 1973.
7. Humanities Curriculum Project, *The Humanities Project: an Introduction.* Heinemann Educational, 1970.
8. E. HOYLE and R. BELL (eds), *Problems of Curriculum Innovation I* (Units 13–15, Course E283 'The Curriculum: context, design and development'). Open University Press, 1972.
9. G. COLLINS, 'The role of the adviser in curriculum change', *Dialogue* (Schools Council Newsletter No. 18), autumn 1974, 14–16.
10. B. MACDONALD and J. RUDDUCK, 'Curriculum research and development projects: barriers to success', *British Journal of Educational Psychology*, **41**, Part 2, June 1971, 148–54.
11. E. R. HOUSE, *The Politics of Educational Innovation.* McCutchan, Berkeley, California, 1974.
12. T. HAGERSTRAND, *The Propagation of Innovation Waves.* Royal University of Lund, Sweden, 1953.
13. T. HAGERSTRAND, *Innovation Diffusion as a Spatial Process.* University of Chicago Press, 1967.
14. J. ELLIOTT and B. MACDONALD (eds), *People in Classrooms* (CARE Occasional Publication No. 2). Centre for Applied Research in Education, University of East Anglia, 1975.

15. *Dissemination and In-service Training*: Report of the Schools Council Working Party on Dissemination, 1972–3 (SC Pamphlet 14). Schools Council, 1974 (out of print).
16. L. J. BANKS, 'Curriculum development in Britain, 1963–8', *Journal of Curriculum Studies*, **1** (3) 1969, 247–59.
17. J. C. PARKER and L. J. RUBIN, *Process as Content: Curriculum Design and the Application of Knowledge*. Rand McNally, Chicago, 1966.
18. J. WALTON, 'Teachers' centres: their role and function', *Forum*, **15**, autumn 1972, 15–17.
19. S. HUMBLE and J. RUDDUCK, 'Local education authorities and curriculum innovation', in *Problems of Curriculum Innovation I* (Units 13–15, Course E283 'The Curriculum: context, design and development'), ed. E. Hoyle and R. Bell. Open University Press, 1972.
20. *Curriculum Development: Teachers' Groups and Centres* (Schools Council Working Paper No. 10). HMSO, 1967.
21. N. EVANS, 'Humanities Curriculum Project and colleges of education', *Education for Teaching*, **81**, spring 1970, 57–62.
22. R. S. FOWLER, 'Humanities Curriculum Project and colleges of education', *Education for Teaching*, **84**, spring 1971, 68–71.
23. D. HAMINGSON (ed.), *Towards Judgement* (CARE Occasional Publication No. 1). Centre for Applied Research in Education, University of East Anglia, 1973.
24. *A Language for Life*. Report of the Committee of Inquiry appointed by the Secretary of State for Education and Science [The Bullock Report]. HMSO, 1975.
25. R. GULLIFORD and P. WIDLAKE, *Teaching Materials for Disadvantaged Children* (Schools Council Curriculum Bulletin 5). Evans/Methuen Educational, 1975.

Appendices

Appendix A Data from the central training courses, 1970–72

Table A.1 Participants at central training courses, 1970

Participants	*Course 1*	*Course 2*	*Course 3*	*Courses 1–3*
Teachers and heads	72	63	63	198[a]
LEA officers	20	15	9	44
Teachers' centre leaders	5	7	9	21
College of education staff	1	2	2	5
College of further education staff	—	—	1	1
Schools Council officers	—	1	2	3
Total	98	88	86	272

[a] Of these 198 teachers, 20 had been engaged in the experiment since 1968. 18 of the 30 LEAs involved in the experimental phase sent teams to these courses; of these, 12 drew on teachers from the HCP teams in the experimental schools. There were 11 experimental teachers at Course 1, 6 at Course 2 and 3 at Course 3. Three more of the LEAs involved in the experimental phase sent teams to the centrally organized but locally held courses described on p. 31.

Table A.2 Staff at central training courses, 1970

Staff	*Course 1*	*Course 2*	*Course 3*
Project team	8	7	8
Evaluation team	2	1	2
College of education staff[a]	1	2	2
Catholic HCP team	1	1	1
Observers	3	—	3
Total	15	11	16

[a] These were drawn from the four colleges that worked experimentally with the Project, 1968–70.

Table A.3 Participants at central training courses, 1970–72[a]

Participants	*1970*	*1971*	*1972*	*1970–72*
Teachers and heads	198	105	119	422
LEA officers	44	4	2	50
Teachers' centre leaders	21	4	4	29
College of education staff	5	7	2	14
College of further education staff	1	2	5	8
Schools Council officers	3	2	—	5
From institutions abroad	—	—	12	12
Others	—	—	6	6
Total	272	124	150	546

[a] Three courses were held each year.

Appendix B Profiles of dissemination in three local authorities

The first two profiles were drafted by the members of the Project and evaluation teams.* Profile C is an account of a dissemination programme that proceeded through sensitive opportunism; it rested on one teacher, by whom the account has been written. (Real names have been replaced by invented ones in the three profiles.)

Profile A Newshire

The local authority, a large county area, offered to participate in the trial phase of the Humanities Project but was not selected. There is a strong tradition of in-service training. The Project is one of many curriculum innovations, both locally and nationally developed, which schools are involved in.

Two of the more senior personnel from a large advisory staff attended a one-day introductory course for the Humanities Project. Since the budget for the next financial year had shortly to be finalized, a rapid decision was made to support local diffusion of the Project. One of the local authority representatives, who had lived and taught in the county for some years, took overall responsibility for co-ordinating local activity, and agreed to deal with financial arrangements, the involvement of schools, the selection of representatives to attend the central training course, and the general organization of local training and follow-up courses. He attended a central training course (one of the first to be run by the Project team), accompanied by the warden from the longest established teachers' centre and by some teachers (one from each of half the total number of schools expressing interest in the Project; they were selected by heads in consultation with the co-ordinator).

This diffusion strategy is close to the one suggested by the Project: a nucleus team centrally trained and with a responsibility for local training, a teachers' centre as a base, and close local authority involvement. Some

* From S. Humble and J. Rudduck, 'Local education authorities and curriculum innovation,' in *Problems of Curriculum Innovation I* (Units 13–15, Course E283 'The Curriculum: context, design and development'), ed. Hoyle and Bell.[8]

teachers travelled long distances for the subsequent training course at the teachers' centre; there were also some college of education staff who wanted to introduce the Project to students.

The local authority undertook to buy materials and essential equipment for all the schools involved and the schools undertook to release teachers for courses and follow-up meetings. Attendance at a local induction course was not a commitment; final decisions about involvement were to be made when the teachers reported their understanding of the innovation to their heads. Nevertheless, all schools which sent teachers to the induction course decided to embark on the experiment. Once the experiment was under way, support meetings were arranged and led by the warden, and held at his centre. These meetings were held in school hours. Some teachers from each involved school attended all the meetings; within a school, teachers took turns in attending in order to reduce the staffing problem. These teachers reported the meeting to their colleagues.

In these early stages, the difficulty, as the warden saw it, lay in sustaining the momentum of meetings and helping teachers to hold on to an experimental attitude to their teaching against the decreasing novelty of the Project and against the increasingly recessive roles played by the warden and the co-ordinator, both of whom felt the pressure of other responsibilities (the co-ordinator, for example, was promoted within the authority). The warden saw two possible solutions: first, he encouraged interest in the possibility of using local materials along with the published materials, and the teachers as a group took advantage of the centre's extensive reprographic facilities to produce their own extension materials. Secondly, teachers from schools not already working with the Project came to the centre to view the published collections of materials which were housed there as part of an information service; as these teachers became interested and joined the regular support meetings, leadership moved from the warden to the long-serving teachers in the group.

Towards the end of the first year of local diffusion the authority clarified its plans for the following year. Schools initially involved were given generous financial support; other schools would have to buy materials and equipment out of their capitation allowance. The authority planned also to involve other wardens in the Project so that there could be established a country-wide network of facilities, with teachers' centre wardens organizing their own series of meetings for teachers in the vicinity.

Profile B Benborough

The local authority is a small, compact county borough which, despite its nomination of one school, was not selected to participate in the trial phase of the Project. The authority has very few advisers (and these in practical subjects only) and no Assistant Education Officers.

The circular letter to local authorities about the Project's programme of diffusion coincided with the appointment of a Curriculum Development Officer (CDO) to take charge of the teachers' centre; the CDO made an energetic response. He attended a one-day introductory course run by the Project team and then visited schools he considered likely to be interested in the innovation. He first approached a school already involved in developing its own humanities course; it proved not to be interested in the national project. He then approached Croxley, a secondary-modern school which was keen to participate. The CDO and a teacher from Croxley (a temporary appointment in the English department) attended one of the first training courses to be run by the Project team. The CDO planned a local induction course and then fortnightly follow-up meetings. He invited a member of the Project team to take part in his local course but pressures on the Project could not allow them to respond where only very small numbers of teachers were involved. The CDO volunteered to open his meetings to interested teachers from neighbouring education authorities where there was no organized local diffusion of the Project.

The CDO bought all the Project materials, as they were published, out of his centre funds, and used them for study at the fortnightly meetings, for circulation among interested schools, and for lending to the one school, Croxley, which was to embark on the Project.

At Croxley, the staffing ratio did not allow the formation of the required small groups of pupils and the CDO volunteered to teach the Project on one morning a week in order to ease the staffing problems and to gain first-hand experience. The Project was located within the English department.

The teachers' centre was the setting for the training course. The warden was familiar with the Project but his role required comprehensive understanding of educational innovation rather than particular expertise, and he did not therefore participate actively in the local diffusion programme.

The support meetings were attended by the head of Croxley, by the school's Humanities team and by teachers from Croxley and other schools who were interested in but not engaged on the experiment. From the start, therefore, the CDO was working with a mixed group of teachers and the meetings were serving as support for the innovating teachers and as gradual induction for other teachers. The meetings were sustained for the best part of a year, largely through the playback and analysis of tapes of humanities discussions.

During the year, the pattern of school activity changed. The teacher from Croxley who had attended the central training course (who was the most experienced humanities teacher) left to take up an appointment at a selective high school in the same authority. He introduced the Project there but neither head nor teachers attended the local Project meetings and the experiment was soon abandoned, partly through examination pressures and partly through inadequate organizational planning. The ex-Croxley teacher then moved to another local authority.

At the start of the second year of diffusion, the Project was firmly established in Croxley (but with only one small group of pupils – the head could not increase the number of groups without increasing their size). The fortnightly Humanities meetings at the centre were replaced by a series of meetings where teachers would be introduced to major curriculum projects concerned with the raising of the school leaving age. The first, which was led by a member of the Project team, was on the Humanities Project. By this time, some schools had bought their own materials and the CDO offered to mount another series of specific Humanities meetings if there was sufficient need. The CDO commented that schools were preoccupied at the moment with secondary reorganization, and that he could no longer be as deeply involved in other projects as he had been in the Humanities Project during the first year of his appointment.

Profile C Broadshire

I came into the dissemination phase of HCP at the time when the Project went public, with the general sale of packs. My training at York, Easter 1970, therefore saw the beginning of two tasks: the one concerning the operation of the Project in my own school, with my own pupils, as an extension of my teaching repertoire; the other, a commitment to introduce other teachers in Broadshire to the Project. I do not know exactly why the LEA suggested that I should attend the York course, for I had done nothing before concerning adult courses, nor given talks in public, nor worked closely with authority officials. I suspect they relied upon my interest in curriculum development, which was apparent in school and in the views I expressed at a local study group set up by the LEA and attended on occasions by advisers.

On two fronts, therefore, I was learning and experimenting as I went along. In some respects this had advantages. The problems anticipated by teachers at courses were sometimes those I myself was experiencing, so I had a genuine interest in helping groups to tease out the issues which they felt important. Also I was anxious to provide the most useful means whereby they might develop an understanding of the Project; so being observant and sensitive to their needs was something I had to develop. Being a beginner myself meant that I had no easy answers for those expecting the 'helpful hints' approach. When experience of the Project grew as a result of my work in school, it became a bit more difficult to appear sincere and yet resist those who would tap my experience as a source of short-term and immediate solutions to their problems. All too easily, demands for hints ('What do you do when . . . ?') could become the trigger for anecdotes. One still feels pressurized by teachers' expectations, [their] wanting the kind of guidance that course-goers are used to receiving. When at HCP courses these expectations are not fulfilled (the goods are not handed out as a package deal), and teachers are put into a let's-work-through-it-together situation, difficulties arise. Some feel disoriented, others frustrated and confused; some find it makes demands on their skills of articulation, on their ability to identify with a group; and some are disturbed by the highly concentrated nature of discussion work. On a recent residential course a very tenacious and involved young man vehemently responded to my question with, 'Don't answer questions with questions'.

Some teachers have been emotionally affected by materials used and views expressed in group sessions. Teachers seem to experience the exposure and uncertainty which can cause anxiety among pupils doing HCP. But, even when the memory of my own training at York had faded, I never had any doubts about the value of the discussion method in training teachers. Moreover, neutral chairmanship, as far as I was capable of it, gave tremendous protection, especially when one was thought to be an authority (even though one might, early on, be hiding a sense of inadequacy!). It helped towards sharpening one's powers of observation and critical faculties – very necessary, if the value of such courses was to be assessed.

Yet, to go back to the early days, I feel that unfamiliarity with organizing training courses may have created a greater burden of work for me, and resulted in less dynamic courses for the teachers. As I gained confidence, I felt more able to make demands upon course organizers (teachers' centre wardens, LEA officers, etc.) which have involved greater expenditure, more complex organization and more allocated time out of school. So that VTR [videotape recorders], visiting speakers, longer residential courses, free materials, have since been included in dissemination courses. At first I felt that everything had to be done by me during courses, and I tended to wait for the LEA officer to approach me when he felt a course should be organized. (This was partly the result of growing HCP commitments at Broadborough teachers' centre.) I also tended to expect that courses and meetings would automatically take place out of school time, at weekends, or in the early evening. Payment was an aspect which was never mentioned, since there is apparently some contractual agreement which prohibits teachers from receiving payment for extra activities within their own area. However, I believe this is under investigation as a result of increasing teachers' centre demands upon serving teachers. However, it was a great help to have an LEA officer responsible for organizing courses, providing facilities, and publicizing details in the schools, and it is no fault of his that the early courses (two days, non-residential) had shortcomings. Like the teachers, and many course organizers, he had experience of other courses where two days were enough to assess the goods, theorize about their merits, and plan classroom application. When I expressed the problems of trying to develop people's understanding of the Project, and he saw the difficulty of organizing support groups with such a geographically dispersed number of schools, he was responsive in terms of general support and finance. My request for a longer, residential course, involving other experienced tutors, materialized for the benefit of a group of twelve teachers in October 1972.

Another Broadshire representative was trained at York at the same time as I was, and together we did two general meetings for teachers in West and North Broadshire. But, being a headmaster, he was unable to take on further work. I was comparatively free to do this, but soon found myself much more frequently involved in HCP work at Broadborough teachers' centre than in my own LEA.

The teachers' centre meetings were all held after school hours, and began with two general meetings, involving around forty-five people. The second of these took the form of an HCP discussion by pupils I was teaching at the time, followed by a general discussion between the teachers and the pupils about the Project. These meetings led to a series of six study groups attended by fifteen to twenty teachers, which turned out to be lively and frank problem-solving sessions (not in any facile, or short-sighted sense).

The main problem there arose from the fact that most of these teachers were regular attenders at all types of curriculum meetings at the centre and were involved in lots of other work organizing Newsom courses and testing Schools Council materials; were heads of departments; were developing examination courses; and had pastoral responsibilities. It is hard to estimate whether they are now able to give time to developing HCP in their schools. Since Broadborough now has only four schools (11–18 comprehensive) perhaps one should be training trainers who would introduce and support the Project in their own schools.

Taking Broadborough and Broadshire together, the courses have involved about seventy teachers from twenty-three different schools. Of those, I think eight schools are still operating HCP, some with variations on the neutrality theme.

DISSEMINATION DIARY, 1970–73

Commitments in Broadshire

May 1970	Two single meetings introducing the Project to teachers and LEA representatives in the area (between 30 and 25 at each).
June 1970	Induction course: 2 days, non-residential (10 schools, 25 people).
November 1970	Follow-up meeting: 'Exams and HCP' (approx. 10 attended).
June 1971	Follow-up meeting: 'Use of film in HCP' (approx. 6 attended).
July 1971	Induction course: 2 days, non-residential (11 schools, 24 people).
December 1971	Follow-up meeting.
October 1972	Induction course: 4 days, residential, with 2 other experienced teachers and a Schools Council field officer (7 schools, 12 teachers).

Commitments in Broadborough

October/November 1970	Six early-evening sessions, introduction and study of the Project for beginners, at roughly fortnightly intervals.

February/March 1971	Rounding off meetings for previous course. Two support meetings for teachers operating HCP. Two general meetings for teachers new to the Project (approx. 32 teachers).
March 1972	'Race and Neutrality': general meeting with a teacher from an HCP *Race* pilot school.

Commitments elsewhere

Easter 1971, September 1972, Easter 1973	Staff member of the central training courses at the University of East Anglia.
June 1972	Three-day induction course, non-residential, at Liverpool.
August 1972	Three-day course, non-residential, in Lanarkshire.
December 1972	Three-hour session at a college of education, Newcastle, as part of a post-graduate course.
February 1973	Talk on chairmanship and neutrality at a teachers' centre in Manchester.
May 1973	Journal article on HCP. Five-day residential course at a college of education.

Appendix C Examples of training-course programmes

Central Training

Residential five-day course at University of East Anglia, Easter 1973

Saturday

Session	Type	Time	Activity
		12.30–14.00	Arrival and registration.
Session 1	P*	14.00–15.15	Introduction to the conference and to the Project.
Session 2	SG†	15.15–16.15	Neutrality and controversial issues. Why neutrality? What is a controversial issue? Should controversial issues be handled in the classroom? What problems are raised by the authority of the teacher? (The early pages of the handbook are relevant here.)
Session 3	SG	16.45–18.00	Discussion continued.
Session 4	SG	20.15–21.30	HCP materials: What is a collection of materials? Using materials in the classroom; storage and retrieval of materials; extending the collections.

Sunday

Session	Type	Time	Activity
		09.00–10.00	FREE TIME
		10.00–11.00	Reading time. A set of accounts of HCP work, by teachers, will be distributed on Saturday evening.
Session 5	SG	11.00–12.30	The Project in schools: discussion of the accounts.
Session 6 and	P	14.00–17.30	Enquiry into discussion: videotape showing problems in discussion work.
Session 7	SG		Consideration of some of the following topics: argument; debate and discussion; pace; discipline of discussion; non-participation and dominance; training the group.
Session 8	SG	17.45–18.00	Preparation for intensive study of materials.
	P	20.15–21.45	Censorship: an examination and discussion of Project materials, including film, that might raise problems in the classroom.

Monday

Session	Type	Time	Activity
Session 9 and Session 10		09.00–12.30	Intensive study of materials. Participants working in threes and fours will review the coverage of a trial collection of materials, in terms of particular issues, and present a constructive critique.
Session 11	P	14.00–15.15	Presentation of reports on materials. Each working group will present the results of its study.
		15.15 onwards	FREE TIME

* Plenary session † Small-group session

Monday – contd.

Session 12	SG 20.15–21.30	Evidence: the nature of evidence and the problems of handling different kinds of material, including visual material.
	21.45	OPTIONAL viewing of films.

Tuesday

Session 13	SG 09.00–10.30	Starting an enquiry: the problem of raising and defining issues.
Session 14	SG 11.00–12.30	Chairing I During three consecutive sessions, groups will discuss issues, using evidence from the published collections of material. Some sessions may be chaired by members of the group.
	14.00–17.00	FREE or preparation for chairing.
Session 15	SG 17.00–18.30	Chairing II
Session 16	SG 20.15–21.45	Chairing III
	22.00	OPTIONAL viewing of films.

Wednesday

Session 17	P and SG 09.00–10.30	Discussion in a context: videotapes of discussion sessions, with excerpts from interviews with teachers and students involved.
Session 18	SG 11.00–12.30	Evaluation: the results of the measurement programme undertaken by the Project's evaluation team.
	14.00–14.30	Reading time. A paper on 'Understanding' will be distributed on Tuesday evening.
Session 19	SG 14.30–15.30	Understanding and assessment: what constitutes understanding? Criteria for recognizing understanding in discussion and non-discussion activities. (Pages 23–36 of the handbook will be relevant.)
	16.00–16.45	Reading time. Copies of HCP examination syllabuses will be distributed in session 19.
Session 20	P 16.45–17.30	The Project and public examination.
Session 21	SG 20.15–21.15	Non-discussion work. What range of activities have schools explored? What are the practical problems? How do these other activities relate to the discussion work? What is the chairman's role in non-discussion work? (Pages 30–33 of the handbook will be relevant.)

Thursday

	09.00–09.45	Reading time. A paper (a profile of the Project in a local authority) will be distributed on Wednesday evening.
Session 22	P 09.45–10.45	Implementation and dissemination: the problems of introducing the Project into schools and local authorities.
Session 23	SG 11.15–12.30	Communication and the Project: the task facing the Project team and the task facing teachers.

a. Non-residential intensive course at the teachers' centre in a county borough authority *

Thursday 30 September

Plenary session 09.30–10.45	Introduction. The course task, RoSLA, curriculum development, humanities, the HCP. Basic Project assumptions.
Plenary session 11.15–12.15	The nature of evidence. The basic oral technique. The role of the chairman, chairing responsibilities.
Study groups 14.00–15.15	Closer examination of Project assumptions, intents and methodology via a study of the handbook.
Study groups 15.45–17.00	Demonstration chairing sessions.
Friday 1 October	
Study groups 09.30–10.45	Chairing sessions by individual members of groups. Analysis.
Study groups 11.15–12.30	Chairing sessions by individual members of groups. Analysis.
Plenary session 14.00–15.15	Outcome work, integration with other courses, further potential, commonly encountered difficulties.
Plenary session 15.45–17.00	Problems of further training and contact, extension of Project methods to other groups. Timetabling and school organization. Examining in Mode III within the examining board. General questions.

Comment by course organizer

The programme seemed to be structured quite well on the whole. In the opening sessions on the first morning the three of us tended to cover the same ground to some extent. This session could have been reduced to one and a half hours; the whole morning was not necessary.

I had obtained handbooks from Heinemann for use by course members but we were short of actual packs to be used in chairing sessions. I managed to persuade our schools to loan two packs for the course but it would be most helpful if either the central team or the publishers would hold a number of packs which could be borrowed for the duration of courses.

The chairing sessions by individual members of groups were most useful and I would regard this as an essential part of any course.

I am following up the course by working with my colleagues in local schools who are using the materials. Some kind of follow-up element in any course seems essential also. Teachers using materials need someone to lean on initially.

* The course (two days, approximately 9½ working hours) was run by the Project LEA contact and by teachers who had worked on the Project for almost three terms.

b. Non-residential intensive course at a teachers' centre in a county authority*

The aims of the course

We cannot hope, in three days, to make teachers fully conversant with HCP materials, nor fully train them in all the necessary discussion techniques. We can hope to introduce materials and techniques and this is an important function of the conference.

Basically, we must concern ourself with attitudes. The HCP cannot be implemented unless the teacher is prepared:

1 to attempt to establish a different relationship (from the traditional one) between himself and his students. In some parts this will be evident in a more relaxed classroom atmosphere and honest interchange amongst all present. The fundamental change will be that the teacher will treat his students as young adults and not as older children.

2 to accept that HCP materials and methods are not definitive; the approach must be experimental with the teacher questioning his approach, use of materials and results at every opportunity.

The aim of the conference, then, is twofold:

a to engender a change of attitude in the teacher in terms of his classroom role and, to some extent, his teaching methods and content so that he will be receptive to HCP methods and materials;

b to introduce HCP materials and methods and give him some experience in handling them.

Tuesday 23 June
10.00–11.30 Introduction: background of the Project and the conference task.
11.45–12.45 Discussion: the school leaver and humanities and human issues.
14.00–15.30 Discussion: the Project approach.
15.45–17.00 Discussion: the Project materials.

* The course (three days, approximately 15 working hours) was run by a fairly large county training team (teachers' centre leaders and teachers) which had been inducted two months earlier at a centrally organized course; no member of the team had had teaching experience of the Project.

Wednesday 24 June

10.00–11.30	Discussion: the role of the teacher.
11.45–12.45	Chairing 1
14.00–15.30	Chairing 2
15.45–17.00	Analysis of chairing sessions 1 and 2.

Thursday 25 June

10.00–11.30	Exams and evaluation.
11.45–12.45	Chairing 3
14.00–15.30	Analysis of Chairing 3.
15.45–17.00	Open forum (including future plans).

c. Non-residential intensive course at a school in a county authority*

Objective of course

To familiarize teachers with the Humanities Curriculum Project, giving them an opportunity of examining and using the materials, and to be in a position to decide whether or not to use it in their schools.

Thursday 6 May, 16.30–19.00
Outline of premises and nature of the course.
The materials and their usage; examination of materials and sale of hand-books.

Thursday 13 May, 9.45–16.00

09.45	Arrive
10.00	Understanding discussion in the classroom: climate of the group; responsibilities and principles of chairmanship; getting the discussion going.
11.10	Head of a local experimental school gives an account of the Project.
11.30–12.00	Group chairmanship practical
13.30–15.15	Group chairmanship practical
15.30	Discussion and feedback
16.00	Close

Thursday 20 May, 16.30–19.00
Group chairmanship practical

Thursday 26 May, 16.30–19.00
Organization of HCP in schools
Activities other than discussion
Drawing together the enquiry: questions and answers (with a member of the Project central team).

* The course (one full day and three half days, approximately 15 working hours) was led by two teachers, centrally trained, who had worked on the Project for almost three terms.

Comment by the course organizer

Criticisms The course consisted of three evenings and one full day and it was felt that three full days would have been better. The evening sessions of two hours were too short. Too often, we had just got into our stride when it came time to finish and therefore we over-ran by three-quarters of an hour on each evening. If we could have provided sandwiches this would have helped those teachers who had a long journey home.

There was no time to use the record player, which would have been valuable.

Film clips would have been most valuable but there was no time to include these; filmstrips too could have been useful. Nor was there time to make use of the material recorded on tape, although chaired discussions were taped, played back and dissected.

More group leaders would have been helpful to enable everyone on the course to act as chairman, though this would have left the groups rather too small.

Only one head and one deputy attended the course and it is vital that the Project should be 'sold' to heads before teachers embark on introducing it into a school. It was therefore felt that more heads should be specifically invited to attend further courses, or better, that there should be one-day courses for heads.

Conclusions The course was successful in that it served as a 'think tank'. It enabled people to think about the premises and to understand the aims of the Humanities Curriculum Project before accepting and attempting to put this Project into practice.

Letters and telephone calls of thanks were received from most people who attended. One comment is worth quoting: 'Even if we never do this [HCP] we learnt a great deal on the course.'

With the lessons learned from this Course it should be possible to run courses for heads and for teachers interested in the Project.

d. Non-residential intensive course at a field centre in a county borough authority*

Saturday 10 April (half day)

am	Introduction	The task of the course
	Discussion	RoSLA Humanities and human issues

* The course (four full days and four half days, approximately 36 working hours) was led by two teachers from the local experimental school.

Sunday 11 April (half day)

am	Discussion	The Project approach
	Audiotape	The nature of enquiry

Monday 12 April (full day)

am	Display	The materials, by Heinemann representative
	Discussion	The materials
pm	Videotape	The Project in the classroom
	Discussion	Analysis of videotape

Tuesday 13 April (full day)

am	Practice	Chairing session 1
	Discussion	Analysis of above
pm	Practice	Chairing session 2
	Discussion	Analysis of above

Wednesday 14 April (half day)

am	Discussion	Organization of the Project in schools 1
	Discussion	Organization of the Project in schools 2

Thursday 15 April (full day)

am	Practice	Chairing session 3
	Discussion	Analysis of above
pm		Films from those recommended
		Films from those recommended

Friday 16 April (full day)

am	Lecture	'CSE Mode 3 and the Humanities', introduction by CSE examinations officer from local committee
	Discussion	Examinations and evaluation
pm	Discussion	Censorship and related problems
	Discussion	Follow-up work

Saturday 17 April (half day)

am		Comments from the groups
		Conclusions

Appendix D Support-group activities

The diary of a local support group, September 1971 to February 1972

The LEA team, an adviser who was based at the teachers' centre (and who kept the diary) and six teachers from six different schools in the relatively compact urban borough, had come to a central training course at Easter 1971. Between April and June the group met four times. During that period they were trying out the Project sporadically in their own classrooms. The Project was scheduled to be taught systematically from September and the team had to work out their strategy for inducting other teachers.

23 September

This was a business meeting which discussed the following points.

a Purchase of films. Mr B agreed to obtain films for viewing, if possible, once a month, the first batch to be concerned with *War and Society*.

b I had been promised a further £150 by Mr H to enable HCP schools to buy storage equipment, and members came to the meeting with some idea of their needs. In the main, schools asked for a filing cabinet (two- or four-drawer) and a three-tiered trolley; these were subsequently provided.

c Because of the difficulty of continuing to find after-school meeting dates which would not clash with other after-school course commitments of members (especially mine – we have a full programme of courses at our teachers' centre) we discussed the possibility of cutting down because of a (commendable) reluctance to eat into teaching time. When I suggested that we could meet after school on Fridays I was agreeably surprised at the almost unanimous acceptance. It was, therefore, decided that we hold film showings on the second Friday of the month, subject to availability of films, and discussion meetings on the fourth Friday of the month.

d We discussed Mr H's proposed CSE Mode III (which has since been approved).

e Information was passed on regarding open days for head teachers and department heads and included in the current Weekly Circular.

30 September

Film-showing: *War and Society*. As in the case of all our film showings, a general invitation to all teachers appeared in the Weekly Circular. The team decided to buy *Protest for Peace* and *Fighting Words*.*

29 October

This was a discussion meeting and the following points emerged:

a Suggestion that there was a lack of humour in many of the packs.

b Fears were expressed of being too authoritarian in the conduct of HCP discussions. Members were often experiencing difficulty in getting much response from their students – in particular, the lack of response to visual evidence was common – and a distinction was made between forcing an answer from students (regarded as OK) and forcing an answer of the kind that the teacher wanted (not OK).

c Mr K gave a lively account of a *Family* discussion with a sixth-form group getting on to the problem of birth control and the Pope's Encyclical, which led to an invitation to a Jesuit organization that one of their priests attend a session to face cross-questioning on the matter. . . . A Methodist lay preacher was invited as a follow-up.

d The meeting then became very heated with battle lines being drawn up as to whether HCP was really 'different from what we have been doing for years'. I don't know whether it was the fact that we were now meeting on a Friday after a crowded week or whether unresolved doubts and misunderstandings had been simmering and had to come out anyway, but all the worries about (and conflicting definitions of) neutral chairmanship and directive *v.* non-directive came tumbling out in unrestrained passion and indignation. (For instance, I found myself abandoning my non-directive chairmanship in order to take up cudgels on behalf of what I was abandoning!)

There were two clear camps. One camp consisted of those who were actually trying to carry out HCP work *à la* Stenhouse or

* Lists of recommended films (from which these were chosen) are included in the teacher's handbook to each HCP pack.

had done so at some time or other, and these were, with one exception, all Norwich-trained; and the other camp consisted of those who were untrained and who were either simply doing social studies in an enlightened-traditional way or were complete bystanders.

Although most people came out at the end flushed with a sort of wild pleasure at having let their hair down (including myself), I did feel immediately uneasy at this abandonment of the supportive nature of the group and blamed myself, not only for having let it happen, but more for being one of the main instigators. I also began to have doubts about the mixed purposes and efficiency of a group which is composed partly of HCP practitioners and partly of non-practitioners, especially since two of the latter are the most vocal and assertive members of the group (see summing-up, p. 154).

12 November

Film-showing: *Relations between the Sexes* (*Crisis*, *Dance with me*, *Feminine-Masculine*). The team decided not to buy any of these films. The only one which got any votes at all was *Feminine-Masculine* but the majority turned this one down too.

26 November

This discussion meeting was poorly attended (a consequence of the battle of the previous discussion meeting – although the intervening film meeting was well attended) and it gave one of our number the chance to unburden her difficulties and sense of inadequacy in conducting HCP discussions with a badly constituted group of reluctant fourth-form girls. Although no one tried to jolly her into a false sense of achievement, it was evident that she was doing better than she thought (I confirmed this when I visited her the following week) and I think this discussion did help.

10 December

This film showing had to be cancelled as Mr B was unable to obtain suitable films in time.

14 January

Intended mainly as a business meeting; the following points were discussed:

- **a** In view of the limited time available to spend the film allocation before the end of the financial year, it was decided to hold a single viewing one Friday evening which would begin at 4.30 and, with a break for refreshments at a local hostelry, go on until 10.00 or so.
- **b** We made some earlier attempts to discuss the possibility of a local diffusion course but these had never got very far. When this matter was raised again in order that a decision be made, it became evident that no one felt that we were ready for such a venture – partly because of our limited practical experience of HCP work, but mainly because the expected increase in HCP participants was too small to warrant a local course. I promised to approach our Deputy Chief Education Officer to see if he would agree to nominate a further group of teachers to attend one of the 1972 Norwich courses on a fully maintained basis (and was glad to report later that he had generously agreed to pay for six).
- **c** The question of the purpose and usefulness of our HCP meetings was raised by one of the members who said that he hadn't attended many meetings because he felt that they were 'a waste of time'. Although this extreme view was not shared by the rest of the group it did serve to bring to light some opinions about the meetings which might otherwise have remained unspoken. There was general agreement that we had spent too much time talking about abstract aims and philosophies, although it was recognized that that was what many members appeared to want at the time and such discussions, therefore, served those particular needs of the moment. It was also agreed that the discussions about film buying had encroached more and more on our limited time. It was agreed that we should postpone further meetings (except for the film viewing) until one or two members had classroom tapes which could again serve as a focal point for discussion.

25 February

The film showing, which was intended to last until 10 pm, took place at the height of the power cuts and, as a result of a general LEA directive, we were not allowed to continue beyond 7 pm. We were thus able to see only a random selection of the fifteen films which had been hired (previously we had been able to get free previews but things had evidently tightened up and we had to pay a hire fee for all the films).

The selection of films was poor – *Friends for Life*, *Naked Hearts*, *Once There was a War* being particularly criticized – and, although *Attention* and *Children Without* would have been purchased *in extremis* we decided instead to buy *Seven Up* and *Four Families*. We also had a preview of the first of the new 'Viznews' series, *The Power Vacuum*, but, although this was interesting, we decided not to purchase.

To sum up, while interest and support have been maintained there has lately been some loss of impetus and a 'losing of our way'. While the fresh group of trainers after Easter should give a fresh impetus to our team (e.g. one of the vocal non-participants mentioned earlier will be of this number) we shall have to try and avoid some of the mistaken procedures of the previous year. I have suggested that film buying should be based on the experience of individual schools who have hired films and tried them out with students (with HCP members also coming to view in the host school); this will save time. As regards discussion meetings, we must try to confine these to practical problems, with or without tapes of classroom discussions. The problem of a mixed group of participants and interested bystanders is a tricky one – one doesn't wish to exclude, especially as this would mark a withdrawal of a previous invitation – and I don't really know the answer. Have you any information on the other support groups which might help?

The London HCP Association

Background

Three of the Project's experimental schools were from the ILEA. The contact for the Project was an English Inspector. In the months preceding the publication of materials and the first round of Project training courses, a series of introductory, or open, days was held at the Project's headquarters at the Philippa Fawcett College, Streatham. Many heads and teachers from London schools attended one or another of these open days and, in addition, a special meeting for them was arranged at County Hall. During the first round of Project training courses a ceiling of ten places per LEA was imposed. The number of would-be participants from the ILEA was greater than ten and so a separate course, five-day and non-residential, was arranged, exclusively for London teachers, by the Inspector. The course was led by two members of the Project team. Thereafter, a sustained programme of induction and evaluation courses was held by the authority at the ILEA residential centre at Stoke d'Abernon. These courses were staffed by experienced HCP teachers in the authority and by the Inspector. At the same time monthly 'follow-up' meetings were held at County Hall. The meetings were convened by the Inspector but eventually resulted in the development of an autonomous association, the London HCP Association.

In 1973 a new post was created in the ILEA for a seconded teacher to work on support for curriculum development and, in particular, the Humanities Curriculum Project. Catherine Berreen, a head of English and leader of a local English centre, was given a two-year appointment. She worked in liaison with the Inspector, Alasdair Aston, who was the Project contact. In time, Catherine Berreen became the acting secretary of the London HCP Association, which worked through a small committee.

The activities planned by this committee, and their own discussions, are evidence of the way a group of experienced and reflective teachers (one was from a college of education) can attempt to carry responsibility for communication and support in innovation. They worked, of course, against a background of local authority interest and understanding – one must not underestimate the energetic contribution of the ILEA through its Inspector.

The extracts that follow are from the minutes of the committee meetings and the notices or reports of the general meetings. They have been selected to give some impression of the seriousness of the concerns that underlie the programme that the Association offers. These are followed by a statement from Catherine Berreen about her work with HCP teachers.

Introducing the Association

1 At an HCP follow-up meeting held at County Hall at 6 pm on Thursday 15 February, 1973, it was decided that an Association of Humanities Curriculum Project teachers should be formed in London.

2 The meeting outlined the aims of the Association as follows:

a To foster an interest in and to disseminate a knowledge of the Humanities Curriculum Project and its related activities.
b To run an Association that was teacher based and teacher organized.
c To provide support for teachers already involved in the project.

3 The meeting further suggested that the activities of the Association should include:

a the provision of 'workshop' sessions for the production of additional evidence;
b opportunities for film viewing;
c the study of HCP and CSE problems;
d the provision of an information bulletin;
e occasional meetings for teachers wishing to find out about the Project;
f evaluation meetings;
g the exploring of possible innovation and development within the Project.

4 The meeting decided to send out a letter addressed personally to all those teachers who at any time have attended an Induction Course for London Teachers, or have attended any of the HCP follow-up meetings or courses. (circular letter to teachers from R. S. W. Skene, first acting secretary, March 1973)

The responsibilities of the acting secretary
The acting secretary of the HCP follow-up group which had been the precursor of the HCP Association had to resign through illness and Catherine Berreen, the teacher seconded to the Humanities support post, took over the role. Her responsibilities were defined by the Committee:

i The minutes of the committee meetings: these should include the points raised, an indication of the amount of discussion, and the decisions made.
ii The minutes or reports of some Association meetings.
iii Keeping a minute book up to date.
iv Arranging some meetings and organizing the circularizing of notices. (from minutes of committee meeting, 13 March 1974)

The future of the Association and other issues

Mr Exton opened the discussion. He referred to the small membership and listed factors which could influence the future of the Association and the place of HCP. These included the fact that there was no longer the publicity of the experimental scheme, that the Project in London had relied very heavily on one Inspector and the courses organized at Stoke d'Abernon, that the Project is very vulnerable to teacher turnover and is difficult to timetable, that it requires a good deal of money. He then said that the Association now had the responsibility for the future of the Humanities Curriculum Project, and asked if the committee's job was to arrange meetings for its small members or to try to appeal to a wider audience. He concluded his introduction by raising the question of being more active, that is, in publicizing the Project and in bringing pressure to bear on heads and on the ILEA. The points made by Mr Exton were taken up and discussed in some depth.

The committee raised the following points: the adverse effects on a teacher's career prospects by involvement in the Project; the role of training colleges; the attitude of headteachers; the use of ETV and the provision of stimulus; the possibility of interesting BBC and ITV in some of the areas covered by HCP; the degree to which HCP has suffered because of other publications in the field of humanities and general studies; and the possibility of opening out discussion of the Project via meetings with the London Association for the Teaching of English, using HCP videotapes. It was agreed that the discussion would continue at the next meeting.

For the time being it was agreed that the committee should apply itself to a greater public awareness. This would mean letters to the press, articles, answering criticisms, getting items in *Education Guardian*. Some specific things were settled – R. Exton would write a reply to Andrew Bethel's article in *Teaching London Kids*, 3, M. Butcher would write an article on the way in which teaching HCP had affected her as a teacher; C. Berreen would contact the committees of other regional HCP associations with a view to organizing a joint meeting, would contact John Bull from Ashmead School about the *Race* pack experiment there and would get Heinemann to state in writing the position regarding future publication of HCP packs. (from minutes of committee meeting, 1 May 1974)

The Association: its constitution and support activities

Election of the committee Discussion of the committee's election underlined the fact that the constitution did not cover such matters as length of tenure. In view of this and other limitations in the present constitution it was agreed that the redrafting of the constitution would take place during this academic year by a sub-committee which would make use of co-opted members.

Any other business There was a good deal of discussion of what the Association should provide for its members. It was agreed that:

a Members should receive one booklet per term containing reports of meetings. These need not always be written by the secretary.

b Occasional papers should be commissioned and sent to members.

c Members should receive copies of the current list of Norwich publications.

d Relevant information from Heinemann re. availability of packs, reprinting dates, etc., should be sent to members.

e Information re. the ILEA film catalogue should be compiled. C. Berreen will compile an annotated list of ILEA films which are relevant to the various HCP packs. This will incorporate the list (already drawn up by R. Exton) of recent additions made on the recommendation of the English Advisory Film Committee.

f Information re. changes in the teachers' handbooks for the packs should be passed on to members. C. Berreen is to do this. (from minutes of committee meeting, 19 September 1974)

Retrospective list of meetings held in 1973/4

27 September 1973

7.00 pm Inaugural meeting including the acting Chairman's report and the adoption of the Articles of Constitution.

7.30 pm Cockpit Arts Workshop. Presentation: *Law and Order*.

18 October 1973

Barry MacDonald, evaluation officer of the Humanities Curriculum Project, gave a report of the latest evaluation findings on progress in schools.

29 November 1973
'How to escape the trap of discussion'
Norah Westlake of Highbury Hill High School and Bob Meadows of Beaufoy School.

11 January 1974
Working session to examine and add to materials in the *Family* and *Relations between the Sexes* packs. Most of the discussion related to the *Family* pack and some material was brought by teachers. As a result of the meeting, lists of information relating to the West Indian background were prepared with the assistance of the ILEA librarian, Jim Wight of the Centre for Urban Educational Studies, and the Community Relations Commission. These and copies of extra evidence used by teachers were sent to members.

28 February 1974
'Film as evidence: some problems'
Jim Hillier from the British Film Institute showed one part of *Protest for Peace* and a study extract from *Les Parapluies de Cherbourg* as illustration for the discussion.

28 March 1974
'Discussion in Humanities Curriculum Project lessons. Can Stenhouse remain pure?'
Videotapes of fourth-year boys at Beckham Manor and of fourth-year girls at Acland Burghley formed the basis of the discussion of the practicalities of chairmanship.

23 May 1974
'Whatever happened to the *Race* Pack?'
Margaret Rogers, co-author of Schools Council Pamphlet No. 9, *Race Relations and the Curriculum*, explained the case that was put to the Schools Council asking for the suspension of the *Race* Pack to enable further discussion of the editorial selection.

27 June 1974
'Group dynamics and the Humanities Curriculum Project'
Peter Whitehouse of the Psychology Department at Philippa Fawcett College discussed recent research in group-dynamics and this was related to discussion in the Humanities Curriculum Project.

Committee meetings were held on:
15 May 1973
10 July 1973
15 November 1973
13 February 1974
13 March 1974
1 May 1974
11 June 1974
15 July 1974. (note circulated to members, September 1974)

The note also included details of the meetings planned for the first term of the new academic year:

1 October 1974
Annual General Meeting followed by 'Starting HCP'. A group of four teachers will describe their experiences as they begin HCP work.

12 November 1974
'Have you done *Poverty* this term?'
Andrew Bethel, a teacher with reservations about the HCP approach, speaks on his article published in *Teaching London Kids*, 3.*

10 December 1974
Extracts from three films of different styles, on the same theme: *A Kind of Loving*; *My Darling Clementine*; *My Sister Eileen*.†

The meetings of the Association were held at teachers' centres and started at 7.30 pm. Notification of all meetings appeared in the ILEA house magazine, *Contact*.

Comment by Catherine Berreen
In the beginning I spent a good deal of time trying to establish the extent of the Humanities Curriculum Project in the Inner London Education Authority. My first impression was of the difficulty of gaining reliable information. This in spite of the fact that I had a list of all the teachers who had been trained since 1970, and so was able to talk to individuals who were in a position to know if the Project operated in their school. However,

* Richard Exton, an HCP teacher, wrote a reply and the two papers were in fact circulated in advance to members.

† It had been agreed that one meeting each term should be devoted to the viewing and discussion of film.

many teachers had moved, even teams of six or eight, including the organizer; and the relation between curriculum development and teacher movement was constantly in evidence. Ambiguity in the use of the word 'humanities' and confusion arising from the fact that in some schools the buying of the HCP materials as part of a resource bank is seen as 'doing the Project' were other obstacles to precise information. My other impression at this stage was of a large number of teachers, not involved in HCP work in any formal sense, who had a tremendous amount of goodwill towards the Project.

In 1973/4 there were twenty-five ILEA schools where HCP was either timetabled or was part of a course such as social education or a humanities Mode III for the CSE. And within these schools teachers felt they experienced considerable difficulties in trying to implement the Project: the status of HCP and the implications of status for staffing and timetabling; the examination question in relation to the aims of HCP; the effect of staff turnover. It is not always easy to communicate to the head and the rest of the staff the nature of HCP work, and without this understanding HCP can become merely notional: the Project might be clear to the team but for others in the school it merges vaguely with other aspects of community or social education, and is therefore vulnerable to timetabling for convenience.

In other schools the concern was with discussion and how it is made worth while for the pupils. A problem for all was that of ensuring regular meeting times for teachers whose main commitment is to another department. Some teachers indicated that they were uneasy about the work, feeling that the Stenhouse approach had broken down and that there was a tension between their expectations and the classroom work; other teachers said quite calmly that the Stenhouse ideal previously informing the course no longer existed, that teachers had moved away from it, though obviously they were much changed and influenced.

I have felt increasingly that the Project has been seen primarily as a discussion course. At meetings of the London Association, for instance, it has been clear that the Project has not been seen as an enquiry. I think that a list of the reasons for this must include the emphasis in the teachers' handbook and the bias of our induction courses. The disenchantment with the Project revealed by some teachers may be linked to this misunderstanding: it is as if their experience of the realities of discussion with fourth-year pupils contradicts what they feel they had been led to expect by Stenhouse and his team, and the induction course.

The question of the difficulty of the materials follows from this. Teachers' comments suggest a certain exasperation with the team because the same difficulty is experienced with later packs as with those published first. It is also interesting that, though the team stated that the packs were to be seen as the basis of a store of materials, teachers point out that they have had to find other materials as if this might be an infringement of HCP or a limitation on the part of the central team. Furthermore I have noted a tendency on the part of teachers whose pupils have spent up to half a term on visits, doing surveys, working in schools or other community centres, and using this experience as evidence in their work, to regard this as in some way breaking with the Project. Was the Project presented to teachers as a static, completed object? Was the Project team unable to convey the implications of being involved in the *process* of curriculum development?

One aspect of my role has been my connection, as acting secretary and now secretary, with the committee of the London Humanities Curriculum Project Association. This has given me some insight into the question of the survival and development of new associations of teachers. The minutes and other matters referred to earlier in this Appendix in no way convey what I term the precarious nature of the Association. The need for the committee to cement and expand the Association is constantly reiterated; there is a concern that the Project be seen positively; and there is a definite awareness that ultimately the committee must be prepared to operate without the kind of support so far provided by the ILEA. The members of the committee also want to prevent the London Association being dominated by a small, inner group. I have been aware at times that I was not part of this group of committed teachers who, with Alasdair Aston, had formed the nucleus of the Project in London, and I can see that it is possible that the very strength of this network may have prevented an opening out of the movement. But the specialist-based organization of the secondary school means that HCP work will form merely a small part of the teacher's timetable, and this must be an important factor in the Association's development.

Appendix E Questions and answers on the Project *

What is the Project all about?

The Project is really about a style of teaching that is often talked about but is less often practised. It is concerned with a learning relationship between teacher and student which is marked by respect for the student's independence of thinking. The Project is best described as a programme of controversial issues, with experimental strategies for handling the controversial issues in ways which will help students to consider a range of view-points and to think things out without being influenced by people, such as the teacher, because they are in a position of authority.

The Project offers the student an opportunity for gaining an understanding, before he leaves school, of a range of controversial issues which are of significance in our society; it offers the teacher a chance to develop new skills and understanding in an area of learning where discussion is the main mode of enquiry.

How does the teacher use this material?

The Project has collected materials to support the enquiry method which it has developed. There are, of course, variations in the way that the materials are used. In the majority of classrooms, the materials are under the control of the chairman who, being very familiar with the materials relevant to the theme the group is considering, will introduce materials into the discussion in order to extend the range of consideration, to challenge or give depth to the views being expressed by the group, or to stimulate a shift to a more productive line of enquiry. The materials are referred to as 'evidence' but the word 'evidence' does not imply particular authority. Any material which is relevant to the issue being discussed is evidence for the examination of that issue. The collections of materials are only core collections; there will often be evidence needed by a group which is not in the collection, and it is hoped that the published materials will be extended and up-dated by teachers and pupils as a result of needs encountered in the classroom.

* The questions were asked by Heinemann's sales representatives and the answers written by JR, Project team, 1972 (see p. 117).

How does the teacher fit into the scheme of things – as a teacher and as chairman?

If by 'teacher' one means a person who imparts information in an instructional way, then that is not the role which the teacher plays in the Project. It would be difficult to justify an instructional position when dealing with controversial issues where people do not agree what the 'right' answer is. Work in the classroom also shows that teachers who attempt an instructional role on a range of controversial issues frequently give misinformation to students. The Project therefore casts the teacher in a different role – as chairman of a discussion group where he has a range of responsibilities: he is responsible for the structure of the learning situation, for ensuring that the discussion is relevant and worthwhile, for seeing that pupils come to recognize standards in discussion and enquiry work, for helping students to plan research and creative activities which will further their enquiry, and so on. He will generally have the collections of materials at his disposal so that he can judge what evidence is required by the group at any given time in order to help them with their task of understanding an issue. It seems that the role of chairman is not an easy one for many teachers to take up: it seems to require a new range of skills. An understanding of what the role implies is best acquired by attending a training course; a full understanding is only achieved through experience with students in the learning situation.

Could the extrovert vocal pupil dominate the discussion to the detriment of the shyer pupil if the teacher remains impartial and does not take part?

There are really several issues in this question. One is impartiality, another is the recessiveness of the teacher, and the third is the handling of a dominant student. First, impartiality: people involved in the Project may tend to use the words 'impartiality' and 'neutrality'. Impartiality is probably best described in the words of a student: 'the teacher doesn't take sides', either with a particular student or with a particular issue. He tries to give a fair hearing to all students in the group and a fair exploration of whatever issues arise. Neutrality is to do with the teacher's own opinion. (The teacher may adopt a role of neutrality in order to see what effects the role has on student learning.) Neutrality would be assumed *because* the teacher is strongly committed on a particular issue and because he *is* anxious lest his commitment should influence the group. Therefore he refrains from expressing his point of view or consciously making it known to the group. In student words: 'he doesn't get in the way of' the discussion.

Another misunderstanding is about the teacher 'not taking part'. The role of chairman, despite the fact that the teacher is attempting to keep his own view out of the discussion, is a most demanding one. The chairman may be active in his helping students to explore evidence (often through the questions he asks), active in trying to understand the points of view being expressed in the group and in matching evidence to the needs of the group as he perceives them. An effective chairman is usually not too recessive.

The third issue is the handling of the dominant student. Dominance is not a phenomenon that is peculiar to humanities work. The chairman has to judge the usefulness of the extrovert student's contributions to the rest of the group. If these contributions are not helpful to the group, then the teacher may have to consider strategies for controlling the dominant student so that shyer or slower-thinking students can participate. This raises the issue: do students have a right not to participate provided that the right is exercised through choice and is not merely the result of shyness or anxiety? The chairman may sometimes choose to invite students to talk about their individual project work in order to give the shyer student something of his own to talk about. The chairman may sometimes need to slow down the pace of the discussion in order to give the slower pupil a chance to contribute.

What department should use the Project?

We cannot say which department *should* use the Project, we can only say which departments *do* use the Project. In some schools the Project is located within a particular department (such as humanities, or English, or history or religious education) but in other schools teachers from varying disciplines form the Project team. Most people would probably agree that the discipline or subject area of the teacher is less important than the teacher's concern to adopt an experimental approach to his teaching. There is one practical problem in not locating the Project within a particular department: the Project enquiry is carried on through discussion and through a range of other activities; these other activities (such as interviewing, going out on visits) sometimes need money, which a departmental allowance would make possible.

Which group of students – RoSLA, sixth-form?

The Project was funded as part of the Schools Council's programme in preparation for the raising of the school leaving age. It was developed with

14- to 16-year-old students of average and just below average ability in mind. Students not competent in reading would clearly have difficulty with the printed materials but, on the other hand, one third of the collections is audio-visual. Some teachers choose to use the approach and some of the materials with students of much less than average ability (taping more of the printed material may be useful in this situation). The majority of schools doing HCP appear to have mixed ability groupings. Some schools choose not to examine everything the students do and here the Project falls into a 'general enrichment' category; in other schools it is part of the examined curriculum. Many schools are now entering students for CSE and of these the majority are working to a Mode III examination. One school has achieved an O-level examination where the Project is part of a fully integrated approach. Once an O-level examination has been introduced alongside CSE, it means that the Project can operate in different mixed ability groups even when the students in those groups are entering for public examination.

Some teachers have introduced the work at sixth-form level but usually as a general topic. We have not yet heard of anyone training students for an A-level examination based on the Humanities Curriculum Project.

Can the teacher miss out the more difficult bits in the materials, or will this 'ruin' the topic being studied?

One of the hypotheses that the Project serves to explore is that teachers' expectations of students can affect achievement levels. As soon as a teacher simplifies, he may be in danger of underestimating the capacity of his students. We have felt that it is important to help a student to work at the limits of his capacity; in other words, to try constantly to extend him. The difficulty level of the materials varies. It appears generally to be higher than teachers are used to presenting to average-ability students of 14 to 16 years.

However, there has been little agreement among teachers about which particular pieces of material are difficult, and some teachers would argue that students are prepared to grapple with difficulty provided that the teacher does not step in to do the work for them. The teacher must of course make judgements about difficult materials in relation to how long the Project has been going: for instance, a group may be less likely to tackle difficult pieces of material or difficult concepts at the beginning of the Project than they will be after a year or a year and a half. It is important to keep the notion of development in mind. It would be helpful to bear in mind also the difference between the two following sequences: 'to read a passage, to understand it and discuss it' and 'to read a passage, to discuss it, and to understand it'. The latter sequence seems to be more appropriate to the values of the Project and in fact more logical. Teachers who indulge in comprehension exercises may find that the significance of the issues under enquiry is lost. Some teachers refuse to interpret some difficult passages on the grounds that the passages are taken from the kind of source evidence which students will meet in their everyday lives once they leave school. It seems to these teachers important that students should not have things simplified at school when they will have to cope with them independently after they have left school. (A helpful analogy might be that of the physically handicapped child whose parents are resistant to doing everything for him lest they prevent him finding out what he can do for himself in normal everyday circumstances; what is at stake is his capacity to become independent.)

Can the packs be used without the films or tapes?

There will of course be variations between schools in the availability of money to hire films, and in the provision of tape-recorders. Teachers who use films tend to consider them very important. For students who do not read a full-length novel, film is probably the only total experience that they can assimilate. Films have an immediate impact: sometimes there may be a danger, in terms of balance, in that the impact of a film which explores one point of view may be greater than the impact of a piece of printed material which is exploring another point of view. It is probably worth while finding out if the local authority can buy films, at least where there are sufficient schools doing the Project to make purchase worthwhile. There is also, of course, the public cinema and television.

Can individual items be rearranged within topics or is there a definite order to be followed?

There is no definite order for tackling issues in any particular enquiry. There is probably a misunderstanding here about the function of the structure in the handbooks. The structure is a map which helps the teacher to find his way through the materials. It represents a logical chart of coverage.

In practice, it is important to find out what aspects of the enquiry the students are most interested to discuss. Teachers will spend some time at the beginning of the enquiry trying to raise with students a number of issues which will provide an agenda. This agenda will contribute some sense of continuity and direction to the enquiry and will also give the chairman a sense of relevance. It also appears important not merely to accept a majority vote on which issues should be tackled first (since this may leave a minority unwilling to participate) but to try instead to find a way of helping students to see that a reasonable compromise among their different interests has to be achieved if the students are to work as a group.

Are any topics more suitable for boys/girls/mixed classes?
There is some evidence that topics vary according to the sex of the group. Some topics may lead boys and girls in a mixed group to take up positions which they think are typical of their sex. The discussion might then turn into an argument between the sexes rather than into an enquiry where individual views may override any sexual difference. In single-sex schools there have been attempts to bring in, for the discussion, students of the opposite sex from nearby schools.

It is very difficult to generalize about topics: it could be that a Humanities group in an all girls school might achieve a broader understanding than girls in a mixed school, who are rejecting issues which they think of as 'masculine'. It depends very much on the relationship within the mixed group to start with and on the teacher's handling of the group.

Occasionally schools have commented on the greater maturity of girls (this will vary in different parts of the country) in handling issues in *Relations between the Sexes*. As always, the teacher must be aware of possible dangers (such as that of a girl versus boy argument in a mixed class, or a tendency towards one-sidedness in a single sex class) and make judgements according to his own situation.

Is there a proper order for the topics?
Again it is difficult to generalize. It seems reasonable not to start a Humanities Project group on *Education* if one knows that the students in that group are already pretty disenchanted with school. Some teachers find *Relations between the Sexes* more appropriate when students are more at ease with the Project style of enquiry and when the teacher is more at ease with the Project style of chairing. It is reasonable to find out what topics have already been handled in schools before the Humanities Project started. Students may well feel that they have 'done' war already.

It is difficult for us to help here since our comments are based on the experience of schools when only four or five packs were published. We have not been able to follow up the use of the recently published collections as 'starter' topics.

We would certainly say that it would be unwise to start a topic which the teacher himself is not interested in or which the teacher feels uncomfortable about handling.

Is there likely to be a syllabus written for HCP? How do teachers evaluate their sessions?
This is a very difficult question to answer briefly. Many schools are drawing up their own Mode III examination syllabuses for HCP. It is difficult for teachers to evaluate development in any new area of the curriculum. There are no established standards or criteria by which to make judgements. It is complicated also by the fact that the aim of the Project is understanding and that understanding, although not an unusual concept in education, is an elusive one. We would suggest that teachers who ask this kind of question should be referred to the Project handbook, to some of the evaluation documents,* and to the booklet on examinations.†

Is any supplementary or additional material going to be produced, or is this all?
The central team is not going to produce any supplementary material. The collections are presented as core collections and it is hoped that teachers and students will add to them as they see the need. They may well wish to add local evidence. In order to facilitate the extension of the packs, the pieces are numbered in sequence but there is a gap of 200 to 300 between each pack. This means that schools which are using the material as part of a larger reference system can add materials and index them in the same way that the rest of the pack has been indexed.

How much teaching time should be devoted to the Project? Does each topic have a definite time limit?
We cannot say how much time *should* be devoted to the Project, only what time teachers *tend* to devote to the project. The average allocation is between four and six periods per week. Some schools prefer a whole afternoon, others prefer two or three double periods, and others a mixture of double and single periods. The allocation of time depends partly on whether the room in which the Project is located lends itself to activities

* D. Hamingson (ed.), *Towards Judgement* (CARE Occasional Publication No. 1). Centre for Applied Research in Education, University of East Anglia, 1973.

† *CSE (Mode III) and the Humanities Curriculum Project*. Centre for Applied Research in Education, University of East Anglia.

other than discussion. It would certainly be difficult to sustain discussion with 14- to 16-year-old students for a whole afternoon without some variety of activity. There is no time limit to any particular topic, but there may be organizational constraints: in some areas the materials are sent around from school to school on a rota system and this means that some artificial time-limit, such as a term or half a term, may have to be imposed.

A topic could go dead on a group in three weeks or less. On the other hand a topic might go on for a year – this has happened in one or two schools. If one has, for organizational reasons, to work to a time-scale then it might be safer, judging from a range of experiences, to allocate roughly a term to each topic. If there are no organizational constraints it is obviously best to pursue the enquiry until it seems that the time is right to finish it. Again the teacher will have to make his own judgements.

Will the contents become out of date?

It is unlikely that the materials will be up-dated. Some of the packs, for instance the *War* pack, were completed before such things as the troubles in Ireland became prominent in national news coverage.

Teachers can, of course, gather their own materials to extend the pack. In one LEA, the teacher's centre leader helps teachers to select articles from local newspapers (he has cleared copyright) and he prints these in twenties.

Some of the Project material clearly will date. Its datedness may not invalidate it as evidence. Other materials perhaps would never be out of date – it depends how one views, say, the Bible, or D. H. Lawrence or Bernard Levin.

How should the materials be stored?

If unlimited money were available then it might well be useful to have a central humanities room, but even here there is controversy in that some schools feel that all materials should be located in the library. In practice it is important that teachers working in the Project have access to as full a range of the materials as possible during the discussion part of the enquiry. If this does not happen, there may be a tendency for teachers to extract a handful of pieces from the total collection, to take these into the discussion, and to ensure that these are the pieces that the students look at even though the needs of the discussion might, if the teachers were able to respond more flexibly, have led them to introduce quite different pieces of evidence.

Some teachers split the twenties into tens and repackage them in another set of polythene bags. Some teachers take the whole collection of materials to their classrooms in concertina folders or in special trolleys (sometimes made by the craft department). One or two schools have bought metal trolleys of the kind advertised in office furniture catalogues.

Schools would be advised to take professional advice on filing systems. We have used the Jolley system.*

Why are there only twenty copies of each item in the packs?

We had to make some decision about numbers. It is important to remember that one pre-condition of doing the Project is the achievement of half-classes. By half-classes we mean no more than twenty students in a group. Ideally, one might well choose to have between twelve and sixteen students in a group. Had we packaged in thirties, there might have been a tendency for half-classes not to have been struggled for. Moreover, if we had packaged in thirties the price would have been higher. There is, therefore, both an educational and a financial implication in our decision to work to a twenty-copy pack.

* An OCCI (optical coincidence co-ordinate indexing) system supplied by J. L. Jolley & Partners, Ltd, Westbourne House, Westbourne Street, High Wycombe, Bucks.

Members of the Project and evaluation teams

Project team	**before Project**	**after Project**
Lawrence Stenhouse *Director* June 1967 – August 1972	Jordanhill College of Education	Centre for Applied Research in Education, University of East Anglia
Gillian Box October 1967 – August 1970	Careers Research and Advisory Centre, Cambridge	Project Information Centre, Schools Council
Ann Cook June 1967 – August 1968	Student, USA	Sarah Lawrence College, USA
Alan Dale November 1971 – April 1972	Astor School, Kent	Astor School, Kent
John Elliott July 1967 – August 1972	Senacre School, Kent	Centre for Applied Research in Education
Pat Haikin (formerly Price) September 1968 – August 1970	Southwark College for Further Education	City College for Further Education
Jim Hillier July 1968 – August 1969	South East London College for Further Education	British Film Institute
John Hipkin September 1968 – August 1971	Research Unit into Boarding Education	Schools Council Working Party on the Whole Curriculum
Andrew McTaggart September 1969 – September 1970	British Film Institute	Hornsey College of Art
Maurice Plaskow September 1967 – March 1970	School Broadcasting Council, BBC	Schools Council (Media and Resources Adviser)
Jean Rudduck April 1968 – August 1972	Brighton College of Education	Centre for Applied Research in Education
Diana Vignali *Part time*, December 1967 – March 1969	Institute of Education Library, University of London	Freelance research

Ron Bland was affiliated to the Project from 1 September 1971 to 31 August 1972 on secondment from Bishop Lonsdale College, Derby.

Evaluation team	**before Project**	**after Project**
Barry MacDonald September 1968 – March 1973	Jordanhill College of Education	Centre for Applied Research in Education
Stephen Humble January 1970 – August 1972	Student, University of London	Institute of Local Government Studies, University of Birmingham
Gajendra Verma January 1970 – August 1972	Department of Education, University of Manchester	SSRC Project, The Problems and Effects of Teaching about Race Relations
Helen Simons July 1970 – August 1972	Student, University of Melbourne	Nuffield Foundation, Group for Research and Innovation in Higher Education